DESTINATION: TRANSFORMATION

A forty-day journey to change the world, written for people with baggage

Anna Townsend

Dedication

This book is dedicated to Bina, my precious sister in Christ, who makes all the work in Nepal possible.

Contents

Where to start, the springboard to change

What is it like to love?

Overcoming

The results are in

And action!

Involving others

Foreword

'Right, guys, I've picked you to change the world.' That might be a crude paraphrase of Jesus' calling the 12 to be His apostles and to be salt and light to the whole world. They also might have seen it as far-fetched, but it happened – they started the transformation. Were they special, godly, mature saints with no baggage? I suspect not: one was a zealot, one a doubter, two brothers described as 'sons of thunder' clearly had tempers, one was too quick to give his opinion, one was a despised tax collector and so on. In fact they were still bickering after three years with Jesus.

We too are chosen and called to be part of the ongoing transformation of His world. Like the disciples, we are not perfect, and we carry baggage. If we are zealous for a single issue, if we doubt we could make any difference, if we sometimes blow up or blurt out, if we are aware of a deep sense of rejection and indeed if we often fall out with others, God still can and will work in and through us, to be part of changing the world. That is His call and will.

It is a privilege to know Anna, the author of this timely book. At one level she is an ordinary person: a wife and a mother of two. At another level she has allowed the Lord to make her extraordinary, which surely is His will for us all. During the time she worshipped at the church I lead in Aldershot, UK, which was not that much more than a year, her Nepalese charity started to flourish and has changed so many ordinary lives, and she started up a local anti-trafficking movement from our church. She could have used her family's frequent relocations as a reason not to get involved in the community, but instead she has trodden the path she lays out in this excellent and helpful book.

Please do read this. Please take time over it and engage with the content. You may feel the needs are too big and you are too small. That's fine, because we can't do it alone. We need God and we need others. He is bigger than the problems and He will use willing vessels.

The best description of Christian ministry I have heard is this: meeting human need, through loving channels, with divine power, to bring glory to God. All four areas are covered by this book: seeing the real needs all around us (and not just those on the surface), learning to feel His compassion and love, choosing to respond and step out in His power to the end that others 'glorify your Father in heaven'. It is not just church leaders who are called to ministry but all of us. This book, if you take it seriously, will help you realise and actualise that call.

Reverend George Newton
Vicar of Holy Trinity Church, Aldershot

Introduction

Does the world need changing? No doubt if you are reading this then you probably think it does, but you may also, like many others, feel overwhelmed by issues and unable to decide which problems to tackle. Could you even make a difference anyway? It is clear that the world is hurting; the good news is that God wants you to change the world. It does not matter if you do not have all the answers or even if you are hurt yourself, you can be used by God to make the world better. Doing so is about allowing God to ignite a fire and passion within you that drives you to love more, make changes and never give up.

This book is written for Christians who believe that not only does God have a better plan for mankind, but that they are called to be part of the answer. It will help you start to transform the world. Being someone who wants to change the world, I often pick up books with similar aims to this one. I read them voraciously, filled with ambition to make a difference, but fail to apply them. So this book is structured differently and consists of 40 daily studies. In sticking to the simple 40-day plan upon which this book is based, the intention is that it will slow you down enough that you are able to take in and apply the daily studies.

I believe you can transform the world, with God's help. Though it takes dedication, it is the most exciting way to spend your life. It will use all your best skills and abilities as well as pushing you on to achieve more than you ever thought possible. This book gives you a simple method to work through that involves daily prayer and tasks so that you will hear from God, discover how God wants you to be involved in changing the world, and work out what your next steps should be. The reading plan lasts for 40 days and should not take up much time on a daily basis; the power of the process comes about through ensuring that the prayers and commitments made through the book are heartfelt and sincere. The thoughts and desires that the book generates should be meditated upon and grappled with so that the reader is constantly bringing them before the Lord.

The process is an amalgamation of two periods of my life; one when I naïvely prayed for God to use me and was then led to set up a charity in Nepal to benefit vulnerable women[1]. At a later stage I was much more intentional about seeking God for the next steps and some of the practical processes and methods I used then are contained here. In combination the hope is that they will establish a spiritual and practical foundation in your life that will enable you to go on to change the world.

Please use a journal to note down your thoughts as you read this book: it will help you to reflect and meditate on your own thoughts and also capture those moments when you get excited about what God is doing in your life. Do not forget those ideas as they will keep you going in the future when the going may get tough. Transforming the world is not easy, but it is never boring. There is also a 'Destination: Transformation' page on Facebook where you can share anything you'd like or ask questions. Please respect the thoughts and feelings shared by others.

It does not matter if you do not have all the answers right now about how the world should be changed, or if you are hurting yourself and are in need of healing. None of us have perfect lives and this book assumes that you bring 'baggage' to the process. It is more than likely that you will experience healing as you are used by God to bring healing and transformation to others. If we come without answers then that allows God to guide us more easily and ultimately brings Him the glory as we know every good thing comes about through his inspiration.

Enjoy your journey with God, as you join Him on the way to a transformed world.

WHERE TO START, THE SPRINGBOARD TO CHANGE

Day 1: What are we hoping for?

This book is ultimately about hope, not only that the world can become better, but that God wants to use you to make it happen. There is no more amazing and satisfying way of living life than one that is given over to God's purposes and in seeing His vision for mankind become reality. The world we live in does not seem to have grasped that hope, though.

Dear Fellow Traveller,

Just a quick glance at my Facebook news feed right now is sufficient to highlight some of many issues that confront mankind today and lead me to feel such despair. My news feed lists articles about modern slavery, orphanage tourism, plastic waste and the destruction of the oceans, homelessness amongst refugees and developing world poverty. Maybe I need to find more cheerful charities and organisations to follow on Facebook, or perhaps, as I suspect, these issues are just the tip of the iceberg and as Christians we should not turn away from them.

Overwhelmed,

Anna

What do biblical hope and a transformed world look like then? The Old Testament prophet Isaiah gives a somewhat abstract yet useful vision of peace and harmony on the earth: 'And the wolf will dwell with the lamb, And the leopard will lie down with the young goat, And the calf and the young lion and the fatling together; And a little boy will lead them. Also the cow and the bear will graze, Their young will lie down together, And the lion will eat straw like the ox. The nursing child will play by the hole of the cobra, And the weaned child will put his hand on the viper's den. They will not hurt or destroy in all My holy mountain, for the earth will be full of the knowledge of the LORD as the waters cover the sea' (Isaiah 11:6–9, NASB). What a picture of reconciliation, harmony, sharing and trust. The weak will be the complement of the strong, and no longer the victim. Any issue I can think of: war, environmental destruction, poverty and many others would be eliminated if these values became reality.

And yet the world groans.

Rowan Williams, the former Archbishop of Canterbury, captures what many of us may feel: 'The cry to God as 'Father' in the New Testament is not a calm acknowledgement of a universal truth about God's abstract fatherhood. It is the child's cry, out of a nightmare.'

The apostle Paul writes in Romans that 'the creation waits in eager expectation for the children of God to be revealed. For the creation was subjected to frustration, not by its own choice, but by the will of the one who subjected it, in hope that the creation itself will be liberated from its bondage to decay and brought into the freedom and glory of the children of God. We know that the whole creation has been groaning as in the pains of childbirth right up to the present time. Not only so, but we ourselves, who have the firstfruits of the Spirit, groan inwardly as we wait eagerly for our adoption to sonship, the redemption of our bodies' (Romans 8:19–23 NIV).

Meditate on this for a moment – the frustration you may feel for the world around you and for the problems you see are not only felt by other Christians, but by creation itself. There is a global yearning and if you feel it, then you are on God's track and thinking like Him. We already possess the Spirit, the down payment and pledge of final redemption, and so we long for the finishing of God's work, described in Isaiah 11 above. Take heart then, this is a sign already that you are in tune with the Holy Spirit, you are feeling what God feels when He looks at his whole creation.

So, it is not wrong to want to change the world, but it is wrong to want to do it on our own and in our own way. We need to listen to the Spirit of God stirring within us and work with Him to make the changes He desires. But that is not easy; finding the solutions is not straightforward, and if you are affected by the very problems you wish to see changed then you may be hurting as well. The world is a messy place and we are messy too, but thankfully God does not veer away from working with imperfect people.

As you work through this book you will find it is especially written for those who do not have all the answers, which in reality is all of us. You may be aware of some things you and others should be doing to mitigate global problems, but I am certain you cannot solve every problem. The good news is that God does not expect us to have the answers. He is the only one who can bring full deliverance and we have to trust Him. You are not the only one to struggle either, so your very difficulty in letting God do His will in your life will allow you to empathise with others who have the same trouble.

Ask yourself

What troubles you about the world as it is now? Can you see solutions to these problems or are they unknown to you? Are you happy not to know all the answers? Are you usually someone who likes to know all the details, are you good at giving control to others? In your journal, write about the areas of your life and times when you have yielded control to God, such as when you became a Christian, and also note down those areas where you struggle to let God be sovereign.

Pray

Commit yourself to partner with God through this process. Pray that He would graciously allow you to be part of healing and changing the world according to His plans, and that you are happy to stick to them.

Day 2: The solution is you

Did you know you are chosen for good works and that God wants to work through you? In fact you and the church are His preferred method for transforming the world.

Dear Fellow Traveller,

My family and I lived in Nepal from 2004 to 2006. Whilst we lived there I struggled with all the poverty I saw around me. My husband and I had gone to live there with the British military (there are about 5,000 Nepali Gurkha soldiers that serve in the British Army and my husband is employed with them). Had we been living in Nepal with a mission organisation or NGO then we would have received orientation training to help us understand poverty and what we could expect to feel living in a third world country as Christians. As a military couple, we were thrown in at the deep end: there was no orientation or course to help us understand the poverty all around us, so we had to wrestle with these issues ourselves.

Kathmandu and another large city, Bhaktapur, both sit within the Kathmandu Valley and there is a ring road that runs around Kathmandu. At one particular point the road from Bhaktapur meets the ring road and there is an enormously wide junction, with countless vehicles, people and animals covering every space. I remember driving through this junction one day – the traffic moves very slowly, of course, as it is so busy – and looking out at all the impoverished people around me. I remember questioning God and asking Him why He allowed so many people to be poor, not only those around me, but all across the world, I felt He was being unfair and I was angry with Him. His answer to me was that He hoped the two billion Christians on the planet would do something about the poverty I saw, and of course that included me doing something. I realised then that we are His hands and feet on earth now and He chooses to work through us to help the poor and other vulnerable groups. It was rather a wake-up call.

Awoken,

Anna

2 Timothy 2:21 says 'Those who cleanse themselves ... will be instruments for special purposes, made

holy, useful to the Master and prepared [by Him] to do any good work' (NIV). What does it mean to cleanse ourselves? Paul further adds in Romans 6:13 'Do not offer any part of yourself to sin as an instrument of wickedness, but rather offer yourselves to God as those who have been brought from death to life; and offer every part of yourself to him as an instrument of righteousness' (NIV). So we need to cleanse ourselves, meaning to confess, repent and turn away from sin and wickedness. Then we also need to offer ourselves to God so He can use us.

The Celtic church has a long tradition of dedicating itself to God's work in the world and serving people, it has a rich legacy of prayers and inspiration on which to draw. There are many profound and weighty prayers that model how to give ourselves over to God's plans.[2] This is St Brendan's prayer and comes at the end of a longer liturgy of adventure and commitment to living on the edge. It is powerful and risky, so read it through first to ensure you understand and comprehend what it would mean for you to pray it from your heart.

Lord, I will trust You, help me to journey beyond the familiar and into the unknown.

Give me faith to leave the old ways and break fresh ground with you.

Christ of the mysteries, can I trust You to be stronger than each storm in me? Do I still yearn for Your glory to lighten me?

I will show others the care You've given me. I will determine amidst all uncertainty always to trust.

I choose to live beyond regret, and let You recreate my life.

I believe You will make a way for me and provide for me, if only I trust You and obey.

I will trust in the darkness and know that my times are still in Your hand.

I will believe You for my future, chapter by chapter, until the story is written.

Focus my mind and my heart upon You, my attention always on You without alteration.

Strengthen me with Your blessing and appoint to me the task.

Teach me to live with eternity in view.

Tune my spirit to the music of heaven.

Feed me, and, somehow, make my obedience count for You.

Ask yourself

Which parts of St Brendan's prayer excite you? Which parts do you find easy to pray? Note those down. Which parts are harder to confess and commit to?

Pray

Read and meditate on St Brendan's prayer. Pray it slowly, line by line, asking God to help you in those parts you struggle with and telling Him about your excitement with the other lines. Pray it again and again, maybe every day for the rest of your life.

Day 3: More love please: how to take the brakes off

The past two days are like the slow climb up to the top of a rollercoaster, you probably knew already that the world is not as God intended and that He wants to involve you with changing it. Now it is time to take the brakes off, you are ready to plummet down the other side and the God-adventure begins.

Dear Fellow Traveller,

This is how it happened for me. I asked God to give me more love for people. It was a simple prayer and I was not very specific about who I wanted to love or why, I just remember listening to someone speak in church one week about how they too had prayed this prayer and how it had led them into ministry with inner city youth. I would never have guessed that I would be filled with love for women in Nepal (at that point I did not know I would be living there), that He would break my heart for them and I would not be the same again.

Changed,

Anna

The words seem so simple: 'please give me more love for people', but they are dangerous words too. Dangerous in a good way, like bungee jumping or jumping out of a plane (with a parachute)!

Loving others like this is to start to feel what God feels about people. He sent His son to die for us and them, so this is no weak, wishy-washy, cute love, this is sacrificial, perilous love that costs. It loves first and asks questions later. We may never be the same again, because our priorities and our mindset will change: the love He gives us will compel us to act and never let us give up until the world is changed.

Perhaps you already know who God will ask you to love or maybe you do not and so you are hoping for a surprise. Please do not rule out anyone or anything, God sees the unseen and He is for them. God sees people that the world tends to overlook, so leave space for Him to reveal people to you that He wants you to love. Maybe you too will soon be seeing the unseen.

When we ask God to give us more love for people, we are asking Him to soften our hearts. There are examples in the Bible of people whose hearts were both softened and hardened, it is a genuine transformational process that God can perform on us and that we can choose to allow.

In Exodus, Moses is commanded by God to return to Egypt and to request that Pharoah lets His people, the Israelites who are trapped in slavery by the Egyptians, go. Yet, God forewarns Moses that 'I will harden his heart so that he will not let the people go' (Exodus 4:21, NIV), and later on God collectively hardens the hearts of an entire people group. Joshua 11:20 states that 'For it was the Lord himself who hardened their hearts to wage war against Israel, so that he might destroy them totally, exterminating them without mercy, as the LORD had commanded Moses' (NIV). We do not want hard hearts like these people, instead, we should follow Solomon's example in his request that God give him 'a discerning heart to govern your people and to distinguish between right and wrong' (1 Kings 3:9, NIV) and David's when in Psalm 51:10 He asks for a 'pure heart' and in Psalm 86:11 an 'undivided heart' (NIV).

It is no surprise then that Proverbs 4:23 tells us to guard or keep vigilant watch over our hearts, depending on the translation used. We are told to do this because 'everything you do flows from it' (NIV). Consequently, if we want to see the world transformed we need to invite God to soften our hearts so that our words and actions flow from it. Love for others from a soft heart will ignite a fire and passion within you that drives you to change the world and never give up or be distracted; the brakes will be off!

Ask yourself

Are you ready to pray this prayer? To ask God to change you from the inside, take the brakes off and enter life with new priorities and passions? Are you aware of any areas where your heart has been hardened? Ask Him to gently soften those areas.

Pray

Ask God to give you more love for people.

Day 4: Being attentive: when does my heart sing?

Having prayed yesterday for more love, you are now open to God moving in your life and revealing to you those He wants you to help. The world is so fallen that He longs for all of us to be involved in restoring it. Your task now is to pay very close attention to acute feelings of love and compassion that you experience. If you get no further in this book than completing the prayer yesterday and the task today, if truly undertaken and made a recurring part of your life, these two will lead you to change the world. It is that simple.

Today begins an ongoing commitment to start noticing and recording the times when you hear, read, notice and learn about something that stirs your heart with compassion, excitement or yearning. What makes your heart sing? What makes your heart ache?

As you continue to ask God to give you more love for people He will activate new passions within you that move you. Take careful notice of these and write them down, in full sentences please! This may seem pernickety, but the adjectives used to describe how you feel may be just as important as the causes themselves. You should write down instances when you feel deeply moved. For example: 'I am horrified by news that human trafficking is happening in my town because a brothel was raided today just a mile from where I live. If trafficking is happening here, just imagine how rife it might be in other parts of the country. I feel awful for the women who have been living and working there for years with no one knowing or caring about them.'

Similarly, there will be times when you feel a spiritual excitement for something such as 'great news that New York City has banned single-use Styrofoam cups, we can save the planet through small revolutions! What's next, New York?'

Do not feel under any compulsion to write down things that make you feel sad, but do not stir you. If a similar incident to the above trafficking raid happens near you, but you do not feel moved by it, then do not write it down. There are plenty of other people and causes God may be inspiring you to care about instead, and you should not feel guilty about it.

Over the next two weeks, as this exercise is carried out on an ongoing basis, you should expect to record between three and twenty-five different instances when you feel stirred. More or less than this is not wrong, but try to keep the list to a manageable size. The world is loud, so try to be selective. On day 9 there is some further guidance for those who just do not feel as if they are hearing God at all.

As you begin to feel deeper emotions for issues you may also start to feel frustrated about the way the world is now: these yearnings and frustrations, if felt deeply, should also be recorded. For instance: 'Meal out with friends tonight was great, but I couldn't stop thinking about the article I read earlier that said there are millions of illegal and underage migrants working in the food industry. It spoiled my meal and I felt as if no one else cared'.

Dear Fellow Traveller,

Looking over my notebook from the time when I kept these notes for the first time brings back vivid memories. This is what started it all and this is what God has called me to. Write as much as you can and enjoy the process.

With excitement,

Anna

If the instances of deep emotion follow no obvious pattern, do not worry either – there are reasons for that too, and when this exercise is wrapped up and reviewed on days 17 and 20, there are options given for apparently disparate spiritual stirrings.

Ask yourself

Are you ready to record instances when you are moved with compassion? How about keeping a notebook/tablet with you at all times? Have there been any times in the last week when you have felt especially moved? Don't drag them up, but if you can remember them easily now then they must have been significant. Record them.

Pray

Go through St Brendan's prayer from yesterday again. Add these words to you own plea for more love as well.

Prayer of abandonment to God[3]

Father, I abandon myself into your hands.

Do with me what you will,

whatever you do, I will thank you,

I am ready for all, I accept all.

Let only your will be done in me,

as in all your creatures,

and I'll ask nothing else, my Lord.

Into Your hands I commend my spirit;

I give it to You

with all the love of my heart,

for I love you, Lord,

and so need to give myself,

to surrender myself into Your hands

with a trust beyond all measure,

because you are my Father.

WHAT IS IT LIKE TO LOVE?

Now we have prayed for more love, will we instantly feel different? This section explains what to expect.

Day 5: When loving overwhelms us

_____

On day 3, you asked God to take the brakes off and to allow you to feel what He feels about people. You asked Him to soften your heart and change your priorities and passions. This was likened to hurtling down the big drop of a roller coaster, an experience that although exciting, can be deeply unpleasant and stomach-churning.

Dear Fellow Traveller,

Before our hearts are softened, it can be very comfortable living in a world where we only worry about ourselves and our immediate family and friends. I liken this to swimming underwater in a warm sea where we can only see a few feet in front of ourselves. When we ask God to give us love and help us to see the world as He does, it is as if we lift our heads above the water and are blinded by the bright sunlight. Though we can see so much more and that may be exhilarating, we may also find that our eyes hurt as the sun streams into them and we feel disorientated, unable to make out what is around us and where we are. The cover of this book demonstrates the stark difference between the two different views. Sometimes I feel jealous of people who appear to me to be living underwater, living a simple life for themselves (of course I do not really know what is going on in their hearts). Life certainly seems easier that way, and trouble-free.

Blinded,

Anna

The needs and hurts in the world are overwhelming, and if we feel even a fraction of God's love for people that hurt, it may overwhelm us almost to the point of devastation or immobilisation. Seeing as God sees is good for us though, and also allows us to see His great hope and love for the world. Matthew 6:22 confirms this: 'The eye is the lamp of the body. If your eyes are healthy, your whole body will be full of light' (NIV).

Some people choose to avoid the news in the hope that 'what you don't know won't hurt you'. Imagine being ignorant of ISIS in Iraq, the Arab uprising, genocide in Rwanda and other human atrocities like human trafficking. That would be a blissfully simple world to live in and it would be much easier to sleep at night. Do not be surprised that as God grants you greater love for people, you will find it harder to assimilate your thoughts and feelings with those of the world and you will feel more uncomfortable.

Love can also manifest itself physically. Depending on the church denomination you are part of there are differing viewpoints on this, about how the Holy spirit works, so you may want to ask your church leader for further clarification on these following points. In my own experience there do seem to be some short term physical side-effects to loving more and it can be good to get wise to what others go through so that you know you are not alone.

There are three main reactions that I have experienced myself and observed in others. First is a spiritual heaviness, which could possibly be interpreted as an anointing presence. I have felt this during worship and it comes just prior to being called to a specific task. Some people may feel compelled to sit, in my case I have to hang my arms down as if to accept the anointing and drop all those things that I know God does not want me to do or hold on to. Sometimes it feels as if I may snap under the weight, but this passes.

Secondly there may be tears of sorrow as our love for others grows. I have seen this countless times as Jesus draws people to himself and helps them to see other people as He does. Jesus himself was described in Isaiah 53:3 as a 'man of sorrows and acquainted with grief' (NASB). In Gethsemane, before He took all the sins of the world to the cross, He was in anguish 'and his sweat was like drops of blood falling to the ground' (Luke 22:44, NIV). Jesus' response to this was to pray more earnestly, and this should be our response too; we should allow the sorrow we feel for others to drive us to God, and not into depression and despair. A deeper sorrow than just tears may also be felt; at times in my own life when I have been made aware of specific cases of shocking oppression and cruelty, then I experience nausea and a sickness in the pit of my stomach. It is as if the news I have just received needs to be expelled from me. *The Message* explains this practical use of sorrow well: 'Distress that drives us to God does that. It turns us around. It gets us back in the way of salvation. We never regret that kind of pain. But those who let distress drive them away from God are full of regrets, end up on a deathbed of regrets' (2 Corinthians 7:10).

Finally, and this may come later when work to tackle problems begins, there is a deep excitement and energy that comes upon people who are called to change the world. As you start to discern your calling, the spiritual excitement you feel will confirm that you are carrying out God's purposes and it will help you to get others involved in helping you. As God works in your life and you begin to feel more acutely His love for people it is all right to ask God to provide you with metaphorical sunglasses so that you are not blinded by everything you can now see.

Ask yourself

Are you ready to feel overwhelmed by God's love for others? Will you remember to use it to turn you back towards Him rather than feeling overwhelmed? Note down any occasions when you have felt overwhelmed or experienced the physical spiritual manifestations explained above. Remember to carry on noticing and writing down those occasions when you feel stirred with compassion.

Pray

Keep on praying for more love for people. If and when you feel overwhelmed ask God to help you through those experiences. Keep returning to Him in prayer.

Day 6: When loving hurts

It is very possible that God is already speaking to you and asking you to help a group of people of which you are part of or that you can closely identify with. You may have experienced the very deprivation or suffering that they do. Of course this makes sense, common suffering and shared experiences unite people and bring about solidarity. They also help to develop empathy and sympathy within ourselves.

Dear Fellow Traveller,

Of course, I do not know what it is like to grow up as an impoverished woman in Nepal, to live within the caste system and to go to bed hungry most nights. Thankfully God has not asked me to experience those things, but He has permitted me to go through some suffering in order to better understand the women the charity helps.

Prior to our Army posting to Nepal I experienced two miscarriages.[4] They were prior to the birth of my first child and when they occurred I wondered if I would ever be able to have children. The miscarriages challenged my faith as I could not understand why God would allow them – I too was comfortably living under the water in my own safe world at this point (see yesterday's notes). By the time the second miscarriage occurred, I felt completely wretched, but during the healing process I came to learn that suffering was completely arbitrary and that those who suffer are not being punished, but are simply victims of our flawed, fallen and sinful world. It was good preparation for working with women in Nepal who suffer greatly through no fault of their own.

Being an Army wife I also know what it is like to be the sole carer for my children. Clearly single parents and those who have been widowed have a better idea of that, but short of being in those situations, being an Army wife can be pretty tough. My husband left for Afghanistan when my daughter was only four weeks old and we had only lived in the area for ten weeks – I knew practically no one. Again, these experiences help me to understand the lives of the women we help in Nepal, all of whom are alone. I can understand and empathise when they choose to live in what we consider squalid rooms but are near to good neighbours who help them with childcare. I can comprehend that a friendly neighbour is more important to them than larger or spotless surroundings.

Having shared both these stories, I still struggle deeply with why God allows so much suffering in the world. It seems so incredibly unfair, and though I believe God is love and He wants only good things for mankind, at times He seems so absent and impotent. I have found that the solution to these questions and frustrations is to keep bringing them to God. Thankfully He does not expect us to have all the answers, and the correct theology, in order for Him to use us and for us to make a difference in the lives of others.

Broken,

Anna

There are some dangers if your suffering has not been resolved yet. Every person experiences suffering differently, and I know of many women who have also had miscarriages, but who years later still struggle with feelings of blame and anger. It is important that we treat every person we help as unique and do not assume their suffering is the same as ours.

Likewise, anger within us, because we have suffered, needs to be rooted out and dealt with. Our anger may be targeted at God or another person who has hurt us. Either way we need to forgive and allow God to heal us. As you work with God to transform the lives of others, you may find healing in the process.

As you ask God to give you more love for others, buried emotional hurts in your past may come to light. Rather than burying them again or becoming bitter, ask God to reveal to you what He wants you to do with those hurts and how He would like you to learn from them. If you are suffering deep feelings of hurt and anxiety about experiences you have gone through, please speak to your church leader or a counsellor before attempting to help others with the same or similar problems. Any festering hurts may inadvertently damage others that you intend to help.

Ask yourself

What suffering have you experienced and what have you learnt from those experiences? Can they be used usefully to benefit others? Are there areas where you still need to be healed? Who could help with that healing?

Remember to carry on noticing and writing down those occasions when you feel stirred with compassion.

Pray

Ask God to help you work through past suffering and to use it for the good of others.

Day 7: When loving is countercultural

If you have ever wanted to be rebellious then, odd though it may sound, loving others is a great way to be so. A recent pop song written by an insightful and eloquent young artist declares 'It's a new art form, showing people how little we care'.[5] Of course, helping others is very acceptable and greatly admired, but our society expects that help only to be given in certain ways. Unfortunately it is not generally acceptable to be full of compassion and love for others and to give them high priority in our lives. Even within a church we can still be expected to fulfil a host of other obligations, for example, helping with various ministries and attending myriad groups, rather than being singular about a cause.

A general rule applied by the world to all people that are passionate about something is that they should not talk about that passion too much; before long they will be considered obsessive. Our culture uses all sorts of negative words to describe people who are fixated by particular things such as 'nerd', or '-aholic' fixed to the end of various pastimes, such as 'shopaholic'. When was the last time you heard a trainspotter being talked about in a positive context? Words like these are used even when the person is not obsessed by something in a way that is damaging.

Dear Fellow Traveller,

A good friend describes the process of coming to grips with some issues as requiring a 'conversion experience'. As an American, she speaks of the need for white Americans to have such an intense change of mind in order for them to understand racism in the country, and to my mind I believe we need to be transformed in regards to our attitude to the environment and climate change. It is no wonder then, that if we undergo such a process of conversion of our attitudes that we feel out of place afterwards.

Out of place,

Anna

Following the prayer made on day 3, you will at first be filled with zeal for some people or cause, which is generally acceptable, but when you do not give up on it, this can be against the grain of our world.

In fact indifference is a key survival trait, protecting us from going somewhat insane. If we were to care deeply about every hardship and form of oppression in the world, we would no doubt be driven to suicide, such is the great level and extent of need. However, indifference is a key cause of continued suffering for many around the world. In Niger, a woman has a 1 in 7 chance of dying in childbirth, even though elsewhere in the world childbirth is exponentially safer.[6] Why does no one act even though the death statistics are so clear? It is because they are indifferent, and in this particular case women's lives are not valued.

Another general rule of society is that if you give money to a cause you should only do so out of your excess, and to reduce or lower your own standard of living and to make sacrifices for others is undesirable. This applies to our time too; if we are perceived as dedicating too much time to a cause then generally society will no longer understand us. If your new-found compassion for people leads you to give your time and money to such an extent that other people perceive you to be compromising your own way of life, then you can expect to experience some sense of misunderstanding and even rejection.

Understanding why the world has these values is vital. As mentioned above, indifference is easy and a certain numbing to the turmoil around us is often inevitable. When we introduce a different way of thinking about others to people we upset their status quo and remind them that there are needs greater than their own. We may make them feel guilty or simply undermine their own worldview and this leads to a sense of confusion and disorientation, particularly if they are without God. The world and its ways are loud, it is hard to ignore it all and as you begin to live with different ethics and priorities, you will find it costly and exhausting. If love is a form of rebellion then the problem with being rebellious is that the novelty soon wears off, and in the case of loving others we are called to be persistent.

Jesus even prayed for us, His disciples, just before He went to the cross, precisely because He knew that His followers would struggle to fit in. He prayed: 'I pray for them. I am not praying for the world, but for those you have given me, for they are yours. All I have is yours, and all you have is mine. And glory has come to me through them. I will remain in the world no longer, but they are still in the world, and I am coming to you. Holy Father, protect them by the power of your name, the name you gave me, so that they may be one as we are one. While I was with them, I protected them and kept them safe by that name you gave me. None has been lost except the one doomed to destruction so that Scripture would be fulfilled. I am coming to you now, but I say these things while I am still in the world, so that they may have the full measure of my joy within them. I have given them your word and the world has hated them, for they are not of the world any more than I am of the world. My prayer is not that you take them out of the world but that you protect them from the evil one. They are not of the world, even as I am not of it. Sanctify them by the truth; your word is truth. As you sent me into the world, I have sent them into the world. For them I sanctify myself, that they too may be truly sanctified. My prayer is not for them alone. I pray also for those who will believe in me through their message, that all of them may be one, Father, just as you are in me and I am in you. May they also be in us so that the world may believe that you have sent me' (John 17:9–21, NIV).

We can see, therefore, that not fitting in has long been prophesied, and should come as no surprise to us who have been called to sacrificially love others. Sustaining our love for others in a world that expects us to act selfishly is not easy and can only be achieved through reliance on God. Thankfully Jesus prayed for us before we were even born and He understands that our lives will be counter-cultural the more we love and value other people.

Ask yourself

Are you ready to be countercultural because of your love and compassion for others? Think about where the pressure to conform to the world's view of life and its meaning comes from in your life. How can you limit their effects?

Remember to carry on noticing and writing down those occasions when you feel stirred with compassion.

Pray

Pray that you would remain faithful to God and to His view of the world. Ask Him to sustain you when you feel as if you do not fit in. Pray for wisdom to identify where pressure to conform comes from in your life and for the strength to overcome it. Thank Jesus for praying for us; He knew just what it was like to be countercultural.

OVERCOMING

Many people set out to love others more, but no sooner than they start, obstacles get in their way. This section is about overcoming those obstacles.

Day 8: Confession

As we learn to love others more, we will at times feel guilty for not loving them sooner; if God is asking us to love unseen people, we can wonder why we did not see them before. Very quickly the Devil can twist our feelings of shame into bitterness towards ourselves and all our good intentions vanish as we are left paralysed by guilt.

Our sins towards others may be because of direct actions that we decide upon and conscious choices that we take that lead others to suffer. It could be that we have chosen to ignore appeals for volunteers at the homeless shelter because we do not want to spend our Friday nights at such a place, or perhaps we decided to buy the cheap chocolate bar knowing full well that modern day slaves and children would have farmed the cocoa used to manufacture it.

At other times we sin through ignorance as we join in systems beyond our control and influence yet which have tangible destructive effects on others. Who can say where the t-shirt we bought last week was sewn together and if it came from a sweatshop? Even executives from our most trusted high street brand names can be duped by suppliers and middlemen who are hoping to maximise their profits and who conceal the working conditions of their employees.[7]

As discussed yesterday, sometimes indifference can seem to be the only way we can survive in the face of so much suffering in the world, yet this too is a sin. At other times we are guilty of acting in ways driven only by our desire to fit in and to please other people. When we live for ourselves and others, and do not put God first, we are also sinning.

Confession is the biblical remedy for guilt and it is deeply and profoundly liberating. No doubt you will have experienced this when you became a Christian. Christ died on the cross for us so that our sins would be forgiven and we would have freedom and everlasting fellowship with Him. Confession necessitates that we concur with God's opinion of us and our sins, it means that we adopt God's view and admit and submit to it.

If you are not used to regularly confessing your sins then it may be worthwhile putting aside some time to deal with past sins.

Confession should also be practiced regularly when we come before God. The Prayer of Examen[8] may be used daily, in the evening before sleeping, to confess sins committed that day to God. It follows three steps: firstly a prayer to prepare and focus on God, secondly a review of the day with an emphasis on thankfulness and reconciliation, finally a petition to God for grace and guidance for the following day. I have found it to be extremely powerful in highlighting recurrent sins in my life and for noticing and attempting to deal with patterns of sinful behaviour. Most people commit habitual sins, they do not often add new ones to their behaviour, and the Prayer of Examen is a wonderful way of developing consciousness of these sins so they can be addressed.

Dear Fellow Traveller,

I have attempted to use the Prayer of Examen in my own life, and it was extremely useful in highlighting to me that I was guilty of committing the same sins day after day. The impatience I often show towards others, particularly my own family, was a recurring theme. I am also at a point in my life where I am aware that I am comfortable with many of my sins, and am much more likely to criticise the sins of others and notice them. My current prayer is that I learn to hate my own sins as much as I hate the sins of others, especially those people I label as bad people, like human traffickers. All sins are abhorrent to God, mine included.

In Christ,

Anna

Richard Foster, in *Celebration of Discipline*,[9] recommends planning three extended prayer times to recall and confess sins from childhood, adolescence and adulthood. After making a list of the sins that God revealed to him during these times, he met with a trusted friend and confessed them. He believes that carrying out this process set him free in ways he had not known before.

Accepting God's forgiveness for our sins, so that we are not paralysed by guilt, is crucial if we want to be part of the solution to the world's problems. The apostle John writes in 1 John 1:5–10 'This is the message we have heard from him and declare to you: God is light; in him there is no darkness at all. If we claim to have fellowship with him and yet walk in the darkness, we lie and do not live out the truth. But if we walk in the light, as he is in the light, we have fellowship with one another, and the blood of Jesus, his Son, purifies us from all sin. If we claim to be without sin, we deceive ourselves and the truth is not in us. If we confess our sins, he is faithful and just and will forgive us our sins and purify us from all unrighteousness. If we claim we have not sinned, we make him out to be a liar and his word is not in us' (NIV). God can be thoroughly relied upon to forgive us and nothing else but the blood of Jesus will cleanse us. We are free then to step forward and undertake God's work in the world knowing sin will not hold us back.

Ask yourself

Are there sins in your past that you need to confess? Can you plan to spend three sessions confessing sins from your childhood, adolescence and adulthood? If you are already feeling led to make a difference to a particular group of people, list any sins you have towards them carefully. Once you have prayed for forgiveness from those sins (as below), destroy the piece of paper; as Jesus said on the cross, 'it is finished'. Consider making the Prayer of Examen a regular part of your prayer life.

Remember to carry on noticing and writing down those occasions when you feel stirred with compassion.

Pray

Ask God to reveal any unknown sins to you from your past. Confess your sins and ask for forgiveness.

Day 9: There is only silence

_____

Since day 4, your assignment has been to remain attentive and record all those instances when your heart has been stirred by love, compassion, righteous anger or yearning. Regrettably, you may have felt none of these spirituals stirrings yet and instead are faced with silence. No doubt you long to overcome that silence and hear clearly from God. Though the task is only five days old, it can be discouraging if your first flush of enthusiasm for changing the world yields no quick direction from God about who He might be calling you to serve.

God desires for everybody to be involved in what He is doing to redeem the world: there is so much suffering and darkness, every one of us is required to be salt and light. God will guide and direct each person who asks Him, everyone is included, but sometimes it is difficult to hear Him directing us.

To help you hear from God through the attentiveness exercise, there are two main ways that you can help yourself to listen. The first is to actively seek out people and issues, rather than waiting for God to highlight them to you as you go about your regular life, so that you can see if your heart is stirred. The second way is to practice spiritual disciplines so that your heart is more in tune with God's. The most effective way to hear God is likely to involve a combination of both methods.

Using the first method to seek out issues requires you to purposefully surround yourself with plentiful sources of information about issues and people that you can reasonably access. This may mean gathering newspapers, books, charity publications and church newsletters. Your local church should publish opportunities to serve people, and if not, ask your pastor to tell you what needs doing locally. You could also commit to watching the news[10] every day and to listening to a talk radio station that discusses news topics. You may also want to listen to some TED talks online and pay attention to what appears on social media news feeds. Once you have surrounded yourself with all this material you can prayerfully and sensitively divide the issues into those you think you may be being called to become involved in and those you do not think are for you. Once you have a set of issues the process can be repeated to further whittle down the list; do not feel guilty about ignoring some issues, instead pick those that interest and excite you. As you identify these, write down what stirs you about each cause. Remember to use full sentences and descriptive words for your feelings as these may be just as important as the topic itself.

All through the ages, Christians have used spiritual practices to draw them into communion with God. These practices are well used and highly recommended, there is nothing particularly strange about them, but if you are using them for the first time it will be worth seeking further guidance about their use, purposes and limitations. They are not magic methods with guaranteed results and each requires perseverance.

Fasting is probably the best-known spiritual discipline, other than prayer, and can be used for the purpose of hearing from God in this exercise, to demonstrate your commitment to submit to Him and your willingness to cast off worldly distractions, including food. Instead of spending time preparing and eating food, why not miss a meal, or several, and devote the time to prayer, Bible-reading and seeking God for direction.

Meditation is a wonderful way to embrace God's truths and letting them embed in your mind. Meditating on scripture, particularly passages that focus on justice and compassion, helps to keep our thoughts in line with God's and to begin to feel as He does about the world. The practice of Lectio Divinia,[11] or 'holy reading', goes beyond forms of meditation you may be more familiar with. It uses scripture as a starting point for a conversation with God through prayer. There are three steps involved: reading the words out loud to let them flow with you, then reflecting on them, and finally taking 'a word' with you throughout the day. Why not start with this passage for your first meditation: 'Therefore the LORD longs to be gracious to you, and therefore He waits on high to have compassion on you. For the LORD is a God of justice; how blessed are all those who long for Him' (Isaiah 30:18 NASB).

Beyond fasting and meditation, there are other spiritual disciplines that help to tune us in to God's voice, these include worship, study, simplicity, service, solitude (more on this on day 14) and celebration.

Dear Fellow Traveller,

Using each of these spiritual disciplines is a wonderful experience in varied and unique ways, I have tried them all to varying degrees. There is definitely a correlation between me fasting and spending time with God, and then life taking off in unexpected ways! By attending New Wine each year with my family I have also experienced the joy of celebrating with others who are also trying to transform the world – I leave envisioned and refreshed spiritually. Just try these spiritual disciplines – you may find God responding to you thunderously!

Expectantly,

Anna

Ask yourself

Is there more you could do to help yourself listen more easily to God directing me? Should you be using one of the methods explained above to hear more clearly from Him? Have you quieted yourself so that you can hear?

Remember to carry on noticing and writing down those occasions when you feel stirred with compassion.

Pray

Thank God for the direction and stirrings you have received from Him so far; ask Him to speak to you more and more clearly so that His purposes can be achieved in your life and the lives of others.

Day 10: Healing my hurts

As stated in the subtitle of this book, we do not need to be perfect people in order to be used by God to transform the world. We may come to this process with all sorts of 'baggage' including hurts and hang-ups. If you are hurting and feel a sense of trepidation about whether your are the right person to be helping others, then even admitting these fears is a healthy starting point. Your pain can be overcome and may provide the key to helping others. Understanding God's character and that He is full of love for you is the foundation for healing hurts.

Dear Fellow Traveller,

I am so very sorry that you hurt. Though I may not know you personally, it grieves me that our world is fallen and full of sorrow. I know that God is sorry too. He is a God of endless love and cares about every aspect of your life. When you hurt He weeps with you and longs to comfort you. He is the comforter and His spirit is one of joy, not sorrow.

The pain I felt following the two miscarriages I experienced has never fully gone away. Sometimes it seems as if I understand why they happened and I am able to see God's hand through it all, but at others I feel a profound sense of sadness as I think about my two children that I never knew.

When the miscarriages occurred, they seemed such random and arbitrary acts that were contrary to the character of the God I once believed in. I wasn't familiar with God as one who permits such pain. I have wrestled with God about why He allowed them to happen and have grown in my faith. He is a God of mystery, no mind can fathom Him, but also the source of the greatest comfort we can ever know. Though it can be hard to reconcile these two aspects of God, and I have by no means done so fully, my understanding of who He is has grown.

With love,

Anna

Psalm 139 contains 18 verses that describe how God not only knows us intimately but cares for us deeply too. It is a beautiful Psalm and a favourite with many. Let these words speak to you: 'For you created my inmost being; you knit me together in my mother's womb. I praise you because I am fearfully and wonderfully made; your works are wonderful, I know that full well. My frame was not hidden from you when I was made in the secret place, when I was woven together in the depths of the earth. Your eyes saw my unformed body; all the days ordained for me were written in your book before one of them came to be' (Psalm 139:13–16, NIV). If God felt such strong tenderness towards you before you were made, then the earlier verses suggest that He will not stop loving you and caring for you when you are alive. The psalmist says, 'You know when I sit and when I rise; you perceive my thoughts from afar. You discern my going out and my lying down; you are familiar with all my ways. Before a word is on my tongue you, Lord, know it completely. You hem me in behind and before, and you lay your hand upon me' (Psalm 139:2–5, NIV).

Suffering is never sent to trip us up, and blaming God for our difficulties, without seeking Him as to why He has sanctioned them, is not worthwhile. By overcoming suffering and sticking with God through life's struggles it proves to ourselves that our faith is strong and that we are overcomers. God does not test us to prove anything to Himself. He knows everything, including how robust our faith is, but often we doubt ourselves. Trials and tribulations produce confidence in ourselves that we are faithful and that our lives have a solid foundation in Christ Jesus. Maybe we did not know this before. Moreover, when we experience the fullness of God's love for us, as John asserts, our fears vanish: 'There is no fear in love. But perfect love drives out fear, because fear has to do with punishment. The one who fears is not made perfect in love' (1 John 4:18, NIV).

If we have suffered at the hands of others, one of the most difficult stages in the healing process is forgiving those people. If you are not ready to forgive yet, then coming to God honestly and pouring out your hurts to Him pre-empts bitterness forming within you. Simply stating to Him that you find it hard to forgive is helpful, and allows His love to be administered to you so that you are able to forgive. In many circumstances it is impossible to forgive through our own efforts, so we need to rely on God to work in and through us to achieve what to us is unachievable.

Our own natures often demand justice too: we desire to make others pay for the hurt they have caused us. Yet the Bible states over and over again that it is God who will administer righteousness and that He will judge. We are cautioned to refrain from overstepping our authority and judging others, especially by using standards we are guilty ourselves of not living up to. We can, however, pray that His justice would be done on earth, and for those who have wronged us to come to Jesus Christ. We are urged to pray for our enemies.

Rather than focussing on your hurt, have confidence instead: at the end of time there will be no more suffering and pain. Our father promises to 'wipe away every tear from [our] eyes' (Revelation 7:17, NIV).

Ask yourself

Have you truly allowed God to show His character to you so that you 'grasp how wide and long and high and deep is the love of Christ' (Ephesians 3:18, NIV)? Have you allowed this understanding to heal your hurts? If understanding isn't enough, then speak to your pastor or a professional and seek help with your healing.

Remember to carry on noticing and writing down those occasions when you feel stirred with compassion.

Pray

Join with the Psalmist and pray these words to God: 'May your unfailing love be my comfort, according to your promise to your servant' (Psalm 119:76, NIV).

Day 11: Letting go of knowing everything

Sometimes the biggest obstacle to us stepping in to help others is our fear that we do not know exactly how to help them. Often we cannot know the precise causes of their situation and to identify how best to help seems way beyond our understanding.

Everyone seems to have an opinion on everything. Even if it is just a 'like' on Facebook or a tweet, it has never been easier to disseminate and share our thoughts. There is pressure to have a view on everything, and admitting that we are not sure about something or do not know about it is thought of as unusual or even abnormal. Daniel prophesies in the Bible about the end times and says that 'Many will go here and there to increase knowledge' (Daniel 12:4, NIV). Whilst not wanting to assert whether or not we are living in the end times, these words seem so true. Knowledge is king right now: we have more than we could ever know at the tips of our fingers on tablets and smartphones, and there is still a great desire to find out and discover more. Our universities are driven by funding and pursue more and more knowledge, sometimes merely for knowledge's sake.

If anything, the great knowledge we have at our fingertips through the internet can allow us as a society to now focus on wisdom, ethics, communication, reason and logic. Our schools could focus on these skills because our relationship with knowledge has changed. No longer do we need to learn dates of battles, names of rivers and so on because we can obtain them immediately on a computer. This is a great opportunity.

The writer of Ecclesiastes recognises how knowledge of a situation can paralyse us from helping. He writes that 'increasing knowledge results in increasing pain' (Ecclesiastes 1:18, NASB). What he means by this is that attempts to solve the problems of life simply enlarge our view of the problem, but do not necessarily bring any solution.

Wisdom is God's solution to this problem, and requires the sensible application of knowledge. If knowledge is knowing *about* something, wisdom is discerning the right way to apply that knowledge to a situation. The Bible puts forward two ways in which we can gain wisdom. First, we can seek it as a gift from the Lord, and secondly, it can be gained through experience, especially if we prayerfully reflect on past experiences. As we approach a problem or seek to change the world we can ask God to grant us wisdom. We should also be unafraid to get involved in a difficult situation, because we know that in doing so we will gain experience that will help us all the more next time we help. Do not expect your help to be perfect the first time.

Of course people have different views on how to apply wisdom in a situation and what to do with the knowledge they have. If, for example, we take the issue of poverty, different political parties, churches and civil society groups will all have different views on what should be done to reduce poverty, and each will cite data (knowledge) to back their positions. In the UK the question of food banks and whether they are good or bad continues to feature in the newspapers. On one hand they are a great example of local churches and communities helping those less well off than them, but on the other they do nothing to address the root causes of poverty and it is questionable whether a well-developed nation like the UK should be relying on handouts to feed its poor. The press asks 'shouldn't the UK be ashamed?'

Knowledge also says that when we help people we should not make them dependent on us. Yet if dependency is to be avoided, presumably independence is the ideal. Who among us though can say they are truly independent? I am dependent on wider society for almost all my needs: my children's schooling is provided by the state, I rely on local supermarkets to have food in stock so I do not need to grow my own, and law and order is maintained collectively. Independence therefore is just an illusion.

Dear Fellow Traveller,

Through the women's charity I run in Nepal, we find it near impossible to avoid making some of the women dependent on us. They have overcome some horrific circumstances such as rape and trafficking and they need our help. We cannot turn them away for fear of making them dependent. We have learnt that the best way to break dependency is to allow them to help others. Yes, they may remain dependent on us, but they are able to pass on their blessings and, if able to choose who and how to help others, are greatly empowered.

Grappling,

Anna

As you are considering where God is asking you to get involved and make a difference, know that there will certainly be times when you do not know what to do or how best to help. What assists one person may hold back another. If wisdom means the careful application of knowledge then we need to pursue both. Read and study as much as you can about the situation you want to involve yourself in. Obtain different perspectives on the problem and diverse views on the solutions. Visit comparable projects or people doing likewise elsewhere and look to see what other countries and cultures are doing to help in similar circumstances. Yet all the time while you are doing this, keep asking God for wisdom to apply what you are learning. Ask Him what He wants you to learn from each piece you read and person you meet. As you start to help and make a difference, keep a journal and learn from your own experiences. What goes well, and what goes wrong? Do not be put off helping because you do not have all the answers.

Ask yourself

Have you been put off helping others because you do not have all the answers to their problems? Are you willing to pursue knowledge of situations and solutions whilst simultaneously seeking God for wisdom?

Remember to carry on noticing and writing down those occasions when you feel stirred with compassion.

Pray

Ask God to help you learn about the issues and people you think you may want to help. Thank Him for the knowledge He has already given you. Ask God for His gift of wisdom to guide you to help others and transform the world.

Day 12: God is in a different time zone

On day 4, you invited God to speak to you and to alert you to the people or situation He wants you to transform with Him. Of course, the timing may not be entirely right for you to start serving these people yet, and you may feel you have not been hearing clearly from Him. The very essence of this book, a 40-day journey to hear from God and prepare yourself to act, is extremely formulaic and may not be right for you, though hopefully it is stirring something within you to seek transformation in the world. While I believe that God has led you to this book for a purpose, and you are reading it during this period in your life for a reason, the time for you to hear and act may not be now. How frustrating! Sometimes it very much feels as if God is in a different time zone to us.

Understanding God's timing in our own life, in the lives of others and for society is a special form of wisdom and is worth striving for. In the book of Chronicles, which contains multiple lists of the 12 tribes of Israel, particular mention is made of the Sons of Issachar. 1 Chronicles 12:32 records them as 'men who understood the times and knew what Israel should do' (NIV). This very simple description reveals much, though. First, the noun 'men' is collective: this was not just one person, but many. If you are struggling to understand God's timing then spend time with people who you perceive to understand God's timing better than you, perhaps someone older than yourself will help you find perspective.

Second, these men understood the times: they were not hidden away, having cut themselves off from the world. No, they were involved in the world and its times. If asked what characterised or was troubling or motivating Israel's people at that time, they would have had an answer. The challenge for us then is to be involved in the world and not be so occupied with church activities that we do not know what is going out there. Reading a newspaper and keeping an eye on popular culture all help, but most importantly we need to have non-Christian friends who can tell us what is going on.

Finally these men 'knew what Israel should do', they seemed exceptionally confident in their understanding. If only that was the case for us! Sadly the passage does not detail how they knew, but it does give the impression that the knowledge was perhaps a God-given gift. The knowledge was not just for them, though, or their tribe, it was for the whole of Israel. Are we seeking to understand God's timing to benefit just ourselves and our family or are we willing to look at the bigger picture and seek God in it?

Dear Fellow Traveller,

As a military wife I move house frequently, and my husband and I have lived in 13 houses over the last 16 years, mostly in the UK but also in Nepal and the USA. Our time in Nepal led to the setting up of the charity that I run, Women Without Roofs, so I have become very spoilt by God, and fully expect Him to use me for His purposes in each and every place we are posted to live. He has been very faithful to me and has never let me down, but on arrival in each new location I am always very impatient to find out what He wants me to do. God challenged me recently by asking me whether, if He were to say that He would not use me until I was 80 years old, I would be prepared to wait. It was not a simple question to answer. Patience does not come easily, but is often required if we are to keep in step with God's timing for us.

Waiting,

Anna

It is worth pointing out that an alternative cause for not hearing from God is that we are the problem. Could you be giving excuses for not hearing from God? Busyness is often cited as a primary reason for not getting involved in doing more, but even if you find yourself in a very busy period of life right now, such as raising young children, there is still preparation you can do to ready yourself for making a difference later on when time is available. For instance, you could research and read about the issue you are called to tackle (see day 26 for more on this), and there is nothing to stop you praying either. On day 19, the need to focus on one issue is discussed, and this too allows more time to make a difference in the area you are called to.

God may also be asking you to wait because of His graciousness. If you are hurt and carrying baggage then God knows exactly how long it will take you to heal. If you feel as if God is holding you back, maybe He knows better and wants to give you time to heal and recover from your past.

It has only been seven days since you begun the exercise explained on day 4. God rewards those who seek Him so I hope you have received some hints from Him about whom He might be calling you to. If it seems as if it may take longer to hear from Him, or if you know that what He is asking you to do will take time to organise (give up your job, become a missionary in a remote corner of Mongolia...), then take heart, the Bible is full of the stories of people who had to wait. Consider Abraham and Sarah, who though promised a son were well into their old age before Isaac was born, also Joseph, Moses and David; some of them had to wait so long that they did not get to see God's promises fulfilled. However, each was faithful in the part they had to play and fulfilled their role in bringing about God's transformation.

There are no shortcuts to God, and keeping in step with His timing is about hearing when and how He wants you to act, rather than achieving rapid transformation on your own.

Ask yourself

Does it sometimes feel as if God is in a different time zone? Why is this? Have you been making excuses, such as being too busy to be used by God? Is there an older Christian with whom you could pray to gain perspective on your calling and life right now? Are you balancing being 'in the world but not of the world'? How are you at waiting?

Remember to carry on noticing and writing down those occasions when you feel stirred with compassion.

Pray

Ask God to confirm to you now about what you should be doing at this stage of the process. Ask Him to clarify whether there is action you should be taking or if your task right now is to wait. If His call on you is to wait, ask Him what He wants you to do whilst you wait.

Day 13: More love again

On day 3, love was described as the engine for achieving transformation both within ourselves and in the world. Very often our love for others wears out and needs refreshing, so today we will apply some pressure to the accelerator and ask God to once again give us more love for people.

The Psalms offer wonderful templates for prayer. They are most often used to inspire worship or as comfort for ourselves, yet can also be used to inspire and stimulate prayer for others. Psalm 23 contains words that appear in many places: on mugs, on bookmarks, and in greetings cards, and they will be familiar to many. Used in the context of praying for others, though, the words take on fresh meaning and in the final section (oddly not usually contained in versions of the psalm that have been put to music) they depict a wonderful picture of restitution.

Psalm 23

1The Lord is my shepherd, I shall not want.

2He makes me lie down in green pastures; He leads me beside quiet waters.

3He restores my soul; He guides me in the paths of righteousness for His name's sake.

4Even though I walk through the valley of the shadow of death, I fear no evil, for You are with me;

Your rod and Your staff, they comfort me.

5You prepare a table before me in the presence of my enemies;

You have anointed my head with oil; My cup overflows.

6Surely goodness and lovingkindness will follow me all the days of my life,

And I will dwell in the house of the Lord forever.

Let us use this comforting psalm to pray for others: use the list you have been writing since day 4 to identify groups. The first three verses are about shepherding – not something many of us in the twenty-first century are familiar with – but they speak of someone who is able to make us feel safe, secure and protected, whilst simultaneously leading us to good new places and ensuring we have everything we need. As you reflect on the different groups of people for whom you are praying, imagine for them how their situation and future outlook would alter if they had such a person to protect them. Of course the psalm is referring to God the Father and also paints a picture of Jesus, known also as the Good Shepherd. Where would He lead them and what would He be protecting them from? As you start to envision good things for these people, pray that these things would become reality.

Verse 4 speaks of God as a companion in our most terrible moments in life. Death is the ultimate root of all suffering, and its shadow is long. Death looms large over those who suffer, either because their suffering will ultimately lead to death, or because death has occurred prematurely and they struggle with the consequences. Death need not only be the physical end of life, but also the death of some part of us, such as our freedom, that we know rightfully should not have been taken from us. Contemplate the others that you are asking God to help you love more; how has death affected them? Has death cheated them of their God-given identity or purpose? Pray that they would be restored.

The rod and the staff spoken of in verse 4 symbolise protection and support. Of whom do you know that is need of protection and support? In what ways could they be protected and supported? Pray that those needs would be met.

Dear Fellow Traveller,

I found the picture in verse five of Jesus honouring someone who had faced abuse and exploitation immensely powerful when praying for a victim of human trafficking.

Women Without Roofs had been helping a lady called Sarda for several years. She had rolled into a fire as a baby and had only just survived; even today she bears the scars of her accident and the skin across her neck, chest and torso is disfigured and stretched. Consequently her parents rejected her because they perceived she was 'a child of bad luck', and so her grandmother raised her. Sarda was married young and gave birth to a daughter and three sons. When her daughter, Sunita, was about 13 years old, Sarda's husband walked out on his family, saying that the scars on his wife's body were too ugly for him to bear any longer. The family was left destitute and when a man promised Sunita a job to help her provide for her family, she was glad and went with him to find out more. Horrifyingly, this man poisoned Sunita and smuggled her across the Nepali border to India where she eventually arrived in New Delhi. She was forced to work in one of the city's many brothels and was beaten if she did not comply; most days she was expected to have sex with at least ten men.

In 2010, I was visiting Kathmandu from the UK and went to visit Sarda; there was a surprise in store for me and our other staff because there was 21-year-old Sunita with Sarda in her room. Sarda had never told anyone that she had a daughter – including our Nepali staff or her pastor – because of the shame she felt. Sarda described how she secretly cried out to God night after night, in the middle of the night, to save her daughter. Finally God had answered her prayers.

Sunita had worked for eight years in the brothels in Delhi, and described to us the hidden rooms behind cupboard doors where she and the other girls were hidden when the police occasionally raided the brothel. She cried as she described the horrific forced abortions some of the girls had endured when they were found to be pregnant. Sunita had eventually run away and worked as a day labourer to pay her way back to Nepal and to her mother. Now she was hiding in her mother's room, unable to go out because of the shame: all the neighbours were gossiping about her and would verbally abuse her if they saw her.

Just to hear her story was harrowing, but to have lived through it is barely imaginable. But when I read Psalm 23:5, I imagine Jesus serving her at a beautifully laid table and honouring her in front of all those who deceived and raped her. They were her enemies, and God chooses to dignify and esteem her while they watch. It is such a powerful picture of restitution and beautiful justice. She is anointed with oil, meaning she is welcomed as He provides lavishly for her; the feast described is no ordinary one. As you continue to pray for others through this psalm, think about who God wishes to honour, and the honour they may have lost through their situation and in their suffering. Pray that it would be lavishly restored.

Still learning,

Anna

The final verse looks forward to a loving and good future and God's promise is that these will continue as long as life lasts. Many who suffer do not look forward to the future, which robs them of hope. Pray that their hope would be restored.

Ask yourself

Can you commit to using the Psalms regularly to help you pray for others? Is Psalm 23 suitable for the people and situations you wish to see transformed? If not, can you find another psalm that is more appropriate?

Remember to carry on noticing and writing down those occasions when you feel stirred with compassion.

Pray

Use a psalm to pray for others. Cast your mind wide as you pray, allowing God to guide you to pray for those He wants you to.

Day 14: Welcome to the wardrobe

This section (days 5 to 15) is about overcoming the obstacles that stop us hearing from God and acting to transform the world. Our world is so full of distractions and temptations that divert and engross us that sometimes it can seem impossible to hear God. Sometimes we need to take more drastic measures to make ourselves available to God and today is about doing just that. You may sit in a wardrobe if you want to.

Poustinia[12] is a Russian word, meaning desert. Deserts in Russia are not like the sandy, hot African ones we commonly think of. Instead they are simply empty wildernesses, devoid of human life and disruption. Poustinia also means hiding place, retreat or sanctum: a place someone who wishes to get away from the diversions of life would go to find solitude and stillness. Not all of us, and not all Russians, have the time or means to take ourselves away: we have responsibilities such as jobs and children to care for, but many Russians reserved a place in their houses to act as a poustinia. It might be a quiet empty room or exterior cabin; if you like the idea of a poustinia, you could perhaps use a cupboard or spare room, its contents should not distract you. I love the idea of being alone and free from distraction.

The purpose of a poustinia is to create a place of quietness and solitude so that God can be heard more clearly. It is very much a place of prayer for others, not a place where we cut ourselves off from the cares of the world. Some hermits would leave their lives behind and go to dwell in a poustinia. They became known as poustinniks and they would take just a few very basic items with them, the only book being a Bible. Upon leaving their home town or village, some poustinniks might have taken the time to say farewell to all their loved ones. Others would just creep away to their poustinia. Would you prefer to announce to your household that you are about to sit in a wardrobe or would you rather just tiptoe off?

Upon entering the poustinia, the poustinik would read only from the Bible and absorb its words into his or her heart. He or she did not take a commentary or exposition with them so they could analyse and distill the meaning from every phrase. Instead, as they read they would let the words sink into their hearts and then have faith that God would make the meaning clear to them. This practice of entering a quiet place, taking only a Bible, and letting the words dwell within us without anxiously seeking their meaning, is one we can copy in our lives. Inevitably we will be stirred to love others more and the discipline will sustain us when we run out of our own resources to change the world.

Dear Fellow Traveller,

In her book Poustinia,[13] Catherine Doherty describes how one can dwell simultaneously in a poustinia and be active in a workplace. This is imminently more practical if sitting in a wardrobe seems bizarre to you. She recalls how Jesus silently worked as a carpenter for many years in Nazareth and how doing likewise can also be good for us and for others. Our very presence in a work situation can be a light to the people around us and can change situations for the better. She says that we ourselves create the space for a poustinia by offering our stilled hearts to be one. Accordingly, if creating a physical place for a poustinia is not possible (not everyone has a spare cupboard to sit in!) then it may be appropriate to simply create a space in our hearts.

Practically,

Anna

Creating a poustinia, whether a physical place or a heart space, is part of the wider practice of simplicity: a discarding of life's distractions in order to be closer to the Lord. Simplicity is an inward desire to be pure that manifests outwardly in our lifestyle. As we draw closer to God inwardly, we find we need fewer worldly goods and so our desire for them lessens. It is an iterative process because once we have fewer possessions and are less concerned by what others think of us, we are able to approach God free from distraction. Richard Foster[14] describes this process as centring; we come to make decisions based on our desire to please God rather than to please others or live up to society's false expectations of us. Simplicity is not about doing without possessions entirely, as an ascetic might, rather it is about gaining a proper perspective on them. By doing so and learning not to worry and toil for things, we leave our minds free to focus on God's Kingdom and serving others. Again, this is part of the iterative process. Focus on God leads us to place possessions in their proper perspective which in turn gives us freedom to concentrate more on bringing about God's Kingdom.

Ask yourself

How you can apply some of the principles of simplicity to your life? What are the biggest distractions that you face? Does it help to spend time in a quiet place alone with the Bible and God? Is there a place you can go to practise being alone and letting God speak to your heart?

Remember to carry on noticing and writing down those occasions when you feel stirred with compassion.

Pray

Ask God to reveal to you things that are distracting you from Him and from loving others more. Ask for the strength to weed those out from your life. Pray that you would be able to focus on God without distraction.

Day 15: Being hopeful

Today is the last that we will be spending thinking about overcoming obstacles to hearing from God and acting for Him. I trust that over the last couple of weeks you will have become aware of people and situations that are in desperate need of transformation and God's love. It can be easy to feel despondent about all the needs of the world and so today the focus is on remaining hopeful and overcoming despair.

There are plenty of verses in the New Testament that tell us that we can hope in God for our salvation, however there is nothing that says everything is going to work out well for us, and the world more generally, during our lives on earth. We know from history that many Christians have died while horrific situations have continued, so as we attempt to have hope for others, we can not falsely believe that everything will be all right. Our hope instead comes from beyond the physical earth and time, and is placed in the eternal God who will judge and who knows everything. As I ponder all the evil in the world, the trafficking and sexual exploitation of children in South East Asia, the horrific killings carried out by ISIS and so on, I can have hope that God knows about every wrongdoing and will not grow weary or tired of redressing them, even though I do. Isaiah 40:28 says 'Do you not know? Have you not heard? The Lord is the everlasting God, the Creator of the ends of the earth. He will not grow tired or weary, and his understanding no one can fathom' (NIV). The Message version puts it more explicitly: 'He knows everything, inside and out'. This is enormously relieving and gives hope in the darkest of situations.

Psalm 46 paints a larger picture of God as one who is able to overcome nations and is more powerful than any natural disaster. Perhaps you are considering some institutionalised sin or act of violence that is too large for any single person to overcome. The good news from this psalm is that God is omnipotent and can overcome any tribulation. Verse 6 says 'The nations made an uproar, the kingdoms tottered; He raised His voice, the earth melted'. Verse 9 goes on to confirm that nowhere is beyond His reach and influence: 'He makes wars to cease to the end of the earth; He breaks the bow and cuts the spear in two; He burns the chariots with fire' (NASB).

Verse 6 is written in the past tense. The Psalmist here is remembering what God has done in the past, it is most likely to refer to the Lord's victory over Sennacherib in Isaiah 36 and 37. Sennacherib, king of Assyria, dared to mock the Lord, and his army was destroyed before it ever engaged the remnant of Israel in battle. We too can use past events to encourage ourselves and should purposefully recall previous times when God has acted in our own lives, or in the lives of others. Take the outlawing of slavery, for example. Just 40 years before slavery was made illegal it was deemed vital to the economies of the UK and Europe. Politicians, business leaders and society more generally believed that if it was stopped then there would be widespread bankruptcy and a worldwide financial crisis. It was an example of institutional sin and suffering, and to almost everyone at the time it seemed impossible to overcome. Yet slavery was stopped, in large part due to William Wilberforce who relentlessly pursued his God-given task, and so we too can have hope in a God who is victorious and can similarly overthrow today's evil systems. Our God never changes.

On day 30, we will look at other role models, but for now let's look further at psalm 46. It only contains two instructions for us in the face of injustice and suffering. The first is to 'behold the works of the LORD' (verse 8, NASB), as we have already considered, and the second is delightfully simple: 'Be still, and know that I am God' (verse 10, NIV). This is not a command to do nothing, rather it is a request to hold firm, to stand still and to rest in the knowledge that God has the final victory. It is a call for us to stop worrying and fretting and to simply let go of our fears. We are not asked to become apathetic or indifferent, but on the contrary to hold onto the high position we have because we know the Lord.

We are not alone when we stand firm like this, and uniting with others to stand against injustice also gives us hope. Each of us is made in the image of God and so it is no wonder that we see goodness in the people we know and together we build each other up. There are promises in the Bible made to groups of God's people that apply to us today too. In 1 Chronicles 7:14–16 (NIV) God promises that 'If my people, who are called by my name, will humble themselves and pray and seek my face and turn from their wicked ways, then I will hear from heaven, and will forgive their sin and will heal their land. Now my eyes will be open and my ears attentive to the prayers offered in this place. I have chosen and consecrated this temple so that my name may be there forever. My eyes and my heart will always be there.'

We can have hope then that groups of like-minded people, in a community such as a church, can pray and see God transform the world. As I write this book, my hope is that you will be called to transform the world for others. Who else can you encourage to do likewise?

Dear Fellow Traveller,

As I look at the pain and suffering in the world I know I cannot tackle it on my own and so I hope to share the burden and inspiration with you.

In solidarity,

Anna

Finally, once we have taken action to right injustices, then Isaiah 58 tells us we can be confident that evil and darkness will be overwhelmed. Verses 8 and 9 promise 'Then your light will break forth like the dawn, and your healing will quickly appear; then your righteousness will go before you, and the glory of the LORD will be your rear guard. Then you will call, and the LORD will answer; you will cry for help, and he will say: Here am I'. None of this happens easily: the rest of the chapter and verses 6 and 7 in particular contain demanding actions that we are to commit to first. These include facing our sins square on, and sharing our homes and belongings with the poor, as well as recognising and addressing injustice. Nonetheless, there is a master plan to bring light to the world and we are already witnesses of the first glimmers.

Ask yourself

Recall a time when God acted in your life and demonstrated His goodness. Are there people who inspire you and give you hope? Can you arrange to spend time with them in the near future? Ask them what gives them the hope they have.

Remember to carry on noticing and writing down those occasions when you feel stirred with compassion.

Pray

Thank God for times when He has demonstrated His goodness. Pray with those who give you hope. Thank God that He knows about every injustice and does not grow weary of doing good.

Day 16: Why not have some more love

Before summing up the results of the attentiveness exercise tomorrow, let us once again ask God to sustain us in our love for others and to recommit to that being the reason for our actions. By now I hope the list that you have been keeping since day 4 has quite a few entries and you have already noticed your love for others increase. No doubt many of the issues on your list will be complex and difficult to understand. There may be obvious perpetrators who are to blame for the suffering of others and comprehending what motivates them may seem unattainable. These people are very difficult to love, yet the Bible is quite clear that we are called to do so. For this reason the focus today is on loving these people, people whom the world may label as evil, crazy or cruel.

Dear Fellow Traveller,

I know in my own heart that I have not mastered loving others who hurt the vulnerable, so I do not come with all the answers today, rather I am a work in progress. As an example of those I find difficult to love, let me describe a situation in East Asia where there is an ill-judged belief that if you have AIDS then having sex with a virgin will cure you. This has driven down the age of girls who are trafficked into the sex industry and many are first sold at age six or seven to 'high class' brothels. Once the girls have been raped for a large price, their vagina is sewn up, without anaesthesia, and they are sold to the next brothel along the chain where they are bought by another man, who now also thinks they are a virgin. This process goes on several times until the poor abused child ends up in a seedy brothel where, her dignity and worth destroyed, she is just one of many young prostitutes.

This barbaric and cruel process outrages me and I feel enormous anger against the men who buy sex from these young girls and the pimps that promote it. I feel rage against the governments of not only the countries where this happens, but also towards my own government; parents sell their daughters because of the desperate poverty that continues unabated in our world. Surely governments should be doing more to end poverty and inequality?

Other than the young girls themselves, I find it near impossible to love anyone involved in this, particularly the perpetrators of this exploitation.

Struggling,

Anna

Jesus' teaching on this matter is absolutely radical: He instructs us to 'love your enemies and pray for those who persecute you, so that you may be sons of your Father who is in heaven; for He causes His sun to rise on the evil and the good, and sends rain on the righteous and the unrighteous. For if you love those who love you, what reward do you have? Do not even the tax collectors do the same? If you greet only your brothers, what more are you doing than others? Do not even the Gentiles do the same? Therefore you are to be perfect, as your heavenly Father is perfect' (Matthew 5:44–48, NASB). His teaching could not be more challenging. We are to love everyone, including our enemies. The men I describe above who buy sex from children are not even my direct enemies, I would find it so much harder to love them if my young daughter were involved and they really were my enemies.

In Luke we are instructed to go beyond loving and praying for our enemies, but to actually do good to them (Luke 6:27). Wow, this is really difficult, but it is in doing good that we start to find common ground. The East Asian men described above have AIDS and are looking for a cure – they are facing their own troubles. Perhaps by helping them acquire treatment for AIDS, ie by doing good to them, it is possible to prevent them from buying sex from children.

It is far harder to love people engaged in oppressive activity if they are right in front of us though, and even more so if they have hurt us. In the example above, the men in South East Asia that are hard to love are distant from me and faceless. I have no need to be anywhere near them unless I chose to be. On the other hand, loving someone who is close to us, who may physically and verbally abuse us, is only possible with God's grace working through us. The Bible says 'We love because he first loved us' (1 John 4:19, NIV). Loving unworthy people who are with us is made possible through the nature of the lover and not the worth of the loved one, it only happens because we have been loved first, by Jesus who gave His life for us in the ultimate act of love.

As we begin to actively love like this, we have to start with understanding ourselves and seeking God, otherwise our anger would prevent us from doing anything to help. On our own, we are incapable of love that goes against our instincts to judge and to feel angry, and so we need to turn to God as the source of this miraculous counterintuitive love. He gives us the qualities and the character traits we need to do this, which are the fruits of the spirit described in Galatians 5:22–23: 'But the fruit of the Spirit is love, joy, peace, patience, kindness, goodness, faithfulness, gentleness, self-control; against such things there is no law' (NASB). How do we grow this fruit? The passage goes on to say it only comes about through walking by the Spirit and not gratifying the desires of our sinful natures.

Loving others that upset us and who perpetrate evil is not easy and requires hard work and patience. We have to rely on God to give us the ability to love them and we are required to wait unwearyingly for the fruit of the Spirit to grow in us: no fruit, real or spiritual, appears overnight. Yet common ground may be found, and just like the example given above, finding ways to heal the hurts of those who inflict pain on others may stop them from causing more pain.

Ask yourself

Are there perpetrators of injustice that you find hard to love? How would demonstrating the fruits of the Spirit towards them help the situation? Are you aware of God's great grace towards you? That His grace saved you? Of how much He loves you now?

Remember to carry on noticing and writing down those occasions when you feel stirred with compassion.

Pray

Pray that you would be able to love more, even when that love seems counterintuitive. Pray for your enemies and for the enemies of others.

THE RESULTS ARE IN

It has been almost two weeks since you began the attentiveness exercise on day 4. It is now time to draw those results together and to find out what God has in store for you. This is the truly exciting part!

Day 17: What have you heard?

Today is one of excitement and anticipation: you will look over the thoughts you have been recording since day 4 and begin to crystallise how God is calling you to transform the world. My prayer for you today is that you are caught up in a clear vision of God's plan for a transformed world and you will never give up pursuing it. Please gather together all the notes you have made since day 4 so that you have them in front of you.

Firstly, let us come to this review with stilled hearts, ready to hear from God. Horatius Bonar, a nineteenth-century churchman describes beautifully how we should come before God to listen: 'It is in the desert that dew falls freshest and the air is purest. So with the soul. It is when none but God is nigh; when His presence alone, like the desert air in which there is mingled no noxious breath of man, surrounds and pervades the soul; it is then that the eye gets the clearest, simplest view of eternal certainties; it is then that the soul gathers in wondrous refreshment and power and energy.'[15]

The Bible gives some detailed accounts of how many people were called by God. These include Abraham, Jacob, Moses, Samuel and Isaiah and it is striking how many of them first had to simply respond by saying, 'Here I am'. We too should begin by presenting ourselves to God and offering our quietened hearts so we can hear clearly and without bias.

'Here am I, Lord, I've come to do Your will.
Here am I, Lord, in Your presence I'm still.'

Now begin to read over your notes, several times. You may have forgotten some of the earlier instances that you recorded, and coming to them now, with fresher eyes, might mean you can more easily distil what it was that stirred you about each case. Record those impressions and any other new ones you may have as you look over the list. On a separate page or piece of paper note down your strongest feeling or stirring as you look at the list.

Return to the list and look for patterns and similarities between your entries. These might occur in the names and nouns you have written. For instance, China might keep appearing, or people with mental health issues, or the name of the town where you live. Look too for names you haven't written, for example all of your entries may be about women, even though you may not have explicitly written the word 'women' down. Write these common names and themes on your new page.

Now look over your original list and highlight or underline all the adjectives (descriptive words) you have used. These might be poor, inspiring, overlooked, ignored, overwhelming, debilitating, big, compassionate, etc. Write down the most common, and what seem to you to be the most significant, on your new page.

With the two lists in front of you, the one you wrote over the 11-day period, and the new sheet you have written just now, consider if the new sheet reflects well the thoughts and feelings you have experienced since day 4. If it does not, then repeat the exercise above. If it does, then wonderful news: you have distilled the essence of what God is calling you to do – I can not promise you will understand it all entirely now, but for some it may be very clear and you may feel excited about what is written on the page.

Dear Fellow Traveller,

When I completed this exercise, the words on my new page seemed to highlight to me how much I did not fit in with other people, I felt as if no one else cared about those things, so why did I have to? My initial reaction was negative rather than excited. However, I did feel as if the words very much reflected my heart for others and, like a mirror, I could see myself reflected in them – deep down, I knew they were my calling. Your feelings about your new page may also be mixed, but please do not worry, tomorrow we will work further on the list.

Feeling different,

Anna

Please remember that just because we are at this stage in this book, you do not have to stop recording and writing down instances that stir, inspire or anger you. You can carry on contributing to your initial list and return to this exercise at a later date. As mentioned on a previous day, although the methods in this book have been successfully used before, the 40-day time frame is somewhat artificially imposed.

Ask yourself

Have you carried out today's task honestly and responsively to God's stirrings within you? If not, where has your own agenda, or the expectations of others, skewed your thoughts? Looking at your new piece of paper, what do you feel most excited about?

Pray

Imagine holding all the feelings and promptings on your new page in your hands and offering them to God. Present yourself to Him again and ask Him to use you to transform the situations you have identified and feel called to. Thank Him for the direction you have received.

Day 18: Focus on listening – tuning in

Today is really a mix and match day, as we consider all the different responses you may have to yesterday's exercise. Hopefully after sleeping on your results, you should feel more settled about them, but if not, then do not worry.

Once again, let us commit to listening to God as we further review the exercise. The Psalmist in the longest psalm, Psalm 119, repeatedly entreats the Lord to reveal His commands and decrees to him so that he can follow them. We can borrow verse 73 and make it our prayer today 'Your hands made me and formed me; give me understanding to learn your commands' (NIV).

You may be in one of several situations following the consolidation of your thoughts yesterday. Your calling may now be completely clear to you, both in terms of who you should be reaching and in what way. For instance you may have been stirred to write down instances where nutrition was an issue for people and you know you are passionate about food anyway. You may also have been inspired by community-building projects you encountered and so the idea of becoming involved in a community-building project using food, such a cooking club for teenagers or new mums, is clear to you. That is brilliant.

Alternatively, you may be clear about one aspect of your calling, let us say you know it has to involve women and interacting socially, but you are unsure about what purpose that should have. In the exercise yesterday you may have felt that you could easily identify the noun element during the exercise, but not the adjective, which would give reason for the transformation God wishes to bring about. The next step for you then is to tune in to God more purposefully when you interact with women in social situations. Your task is to repeat the attentiveness exercise again, but this time to focus on the stirrings you notice chiefly when you are with women socially. Do you feel strongly about inclusivity? Are you perhaps drawn to women who have suffered from depression? What is it about interacting socially with other women that you feel is important? How is it good for you and others? As you focus on answering and noticing more specifically regarding your broader calling, you will be able to focus in on what God has prepared for you to do. Again, give yourself approximately two weeks to repeat this more specific exercise.

In a third group, there will be those of you who have a very clear calling to a particular cause, usually identified by the adjective part of the exercise yesterday, but do not know with whom or where to address that issue. For example, words such as inequality, poverty, economic injustice, poor, etc, may have appeared repeatedly over the last couple of weeks. Your task is also to repeat the attentiveness exercise, focusing only on this theme. Try to notice where your life and daily routine intersect with the poor. Is your church already working with the poor? Are you mainly concerned with the poor overseas or does local poverty produce stronger feelings in you? Again, give yourself two weeks to redo the exercise with this specific focus.

Finally, there will be those who feel no clear calling from God about anything yet, and this too is fine. If you are not feeling stirred by anything, then keep going with the original exercise, as explained on day 4, and read through the 'overcoming' pages on days 5 to 15 again. If you did not do so before, consider spending a day fasting or on your own, to clear away distractions and to hear plainly from the Lord. Alternatively, you may be feeling overwhelmed and stirred to action by everything you hear about; in this case you should find day 20 ('What if there is a cacophony?') helpful.

Dear Fellow Traveller,

In my own case, when I carried out this exercise, the words that struck me were global, compassion, unseen, and transformation (hence the title of this book). Initially, as I explained yesterday, I felt these words marked me out as different and epitomised why I did not fit in with other people – I was the mother of two young children at the time and everybody else seemed to spend their time talking about nurseries and nappies.

I had a deep experience at church one day where a lot of people were going to the front to share stories of how God had done something for them that week, like fix their leaky tap, and all I could do was feel profoundly depressed about everything that was going on in Syria at that time. I suppose I yearned for my heart to be focussed a little less on global problems and more about the ordinary, so I spent the next few weeks paying attention to when my heart was stirred by global themes. In time, I came to see that my broader view was God-given and that He was calling me to think about global issues and was going to use me to work across borders. I now treasure my ability to think globally, observe global movements and have been fortunate to live overseas twice. I would not be able to run a charity in Nepal without this perspective and I am now also involved in other committees that are concerned with Asia and work with refugees.

At peace,

Anna

However you feel about your calling right now, my prayer is that you will come to love and embrace it, and view it as uniquely given to you. I pray that opportunities to make a difference in the areas you have identified and to see them transformed will quickly become apparent to you.

Ask yourself

Is your calling becoming clearer? What actions can you take to crystallise it? How do you feel about your calling? What can you do to treasure that calling as God does?

Pray

Thank God for the calling on your life that you have discerned so far. Ask Him to keep on clarifying it and to give you opportunities to respond to your calling so that the world can be transformed.

Day 19: Just choose one – abandon and obey

_____

As I said on day 3, the secret to transforming the world is doing so out of deep, compassionate love. The second key to seeing societal transformation is being devoted to that issue, sometimes to the exclusion of others. Most great world-changers (we will discuss some examples of role models when we reach day 30) are, or were, uncompromisingly committed to the issues they are called to; they often do not spread themselves too thin trying to change everything and everyone.

Having heard from God what it is He is calling you to do over the past two days, the decision rests with you as to whether you are going to pursue it wholeheartedly or if you will commit to a smorgasbord of issues. There is no right or wrong way, other than to seek God to guide you, but if you believe God is clearly calling you to transform His world then now is the time to abandon everything else, to clear your diary and your task list, and commit to one people group or issue.

Dear Fellow Traveller,

The suggestion is not that you suddenly ditch and let down people who are relying on you, but over a period of a few months it should be possible to prayerfully narrow down your existing commitments and hand over tasks to others. You should, of course, retain your commitment to things that are related to your calling. How extreme you are in weeding out tasks is a matter of judgement and wisdom. Ask for advice from someone you trust to help you discard the unnecessary, but keep those things that will not stop you from being devoted to your calling. For instance, I still help out in Sunday school, even though I know it is not an integral part of my drive to change the world, because I know it is useful and helpful to my church. There are many others for whom helping the young people in their church is a key part of their calling. That is brilliant, we are each called to different groups and purposes.

Cautiously,

Anna

Then comes the exciting part. You need to obey and say yes to every opportunity and person that comes along which is related to the issue that has been revealed to you. For those that were hoping for some spare time, then it may be that initially, after your weeding-out phase, you will have some. However, as you say yes and explore opportunities, you may soon find your diary fills up again with new groups and people. This time, however, they will each be related to your mission to transform the world. Achieving this single-mindedness will help your time management and give you a sense of control over what you are involved in; something many Christians long for. Saying no to something that you obviously feel no passion for will be easier and because you will be able to sensibly justify it, you should experience no guilt over saying no.

Test every opportunity that comes your way against the words that you have narrowed down and identified over the past two days, and if there is a connection, pursue it. Arrange to meet as many people as you can who are involved in the issue you care about, ideally in a one-to-one setting so that you can ask questions. You will be able to make connections between each of the people you meet, and work more effectively on your cause because you will have a wider network to draw on and learn from. In my case I always try to meet up with anyone I come across who is working in or has a connection to Nepal. The consequence of this approach is that even though Women Without Roofs focuses solely on women that are on their own in Kathmandu, I have a wide range of contacts working in different regions of Nepal and others who can help me with issues relating to mental health, human trafficking, biodynamic farming, the persecution of Christians, sustainable business start up and tourism, amongst many other matters.

At different phases of our life, being singular and focused on one particular cause like this is met with more acceptance than at other times. Teenagers that refuse to settle for how things are and have great drive to change the world are typically viewed favourably and their ambition is accepted and encouraged. Indeed these characteristics are celebrated in much of teen culture, and to be a teenage rebel with a cause is nothing new and has been the subject of many films. To have those same feelings in middle-age and old-age conversely can be judged by others to be a sign of a 'midlife crisis', by then we are expected to accept life the way it is and to mostly give up on our ambitions. Yet God excludes no one from His great plan to transform the world and involves all of us in doing so, there are no age barriers. God loves old and middle-age rebels with causes!

Returning again to Romans 8 (see day 1) we read that the whole of creation and each and every one of us is groaning for redemption and to be freed from corruption; this spiritual groaning is not experienced only by those who are young. Joel 2:28 confirms that the Holy Spirit is poured out on each of us 'And afterwards, I will pour out my Spirit on all people. Your sons and daughters will prophesy, your old men will dream dreams, your young men will see visions' (NIV). The Spirit spoken of here is one of prophecy and the ability to see situations through God's eyes, it is one that inspires and hopes for a great future and everyone will be included in seeing and desiring it. No one is too old to yearn for a hopeful future and to resolutely pursue it through dedicating their life to it, no matter how much or how little of their life remains.

Ask yourself

Are you willing to commit wholeheartedly to a distinct issue and pursue it single-mindedly? Can you discern which commitments, roles or tasks you should give up and which you should hold on to? Are there new opportunities you need to say yes to? Have you wrongfully let your age dictate your spiritual desires and yearnings?

Pray

Ask God to reveal to you those areas that He wants you to step back from and those He wants you to take up. Pray for wisdom to sensitively hand things over to others. Ask for new opportunities related to your calling.

Day 20: What if there is a cacophony?

Today is written for those who have found the past few days difficult, who found it impossible to narrow down a large list of spiritual stirrings on days 17 and 18, and who were horrified at the idea of being single-minded yesterday. These people, when they pray about the world, will experience a barrage of thoughts about what needs to change and will hear a cacophony, like deafening alarm bells, of ideas from God about what needs to be done. The good news is that there are roles and purposes for people who are called like this; God has great plans for people who care about multiple issues, and today we will explore several options for pursuing a calling to numerous subjects. My belief though is that most people are called to narrow down the causes they focus on and greatest transformation will occur when people are single-minded. Let's proceed though, because some readers will be hearing a cacophony from God right now.

First, there are those who are not called to lead and pioneer on a particular issue. Instead these people are encouragers who support, serve and back other people who have callings to lead. I have huge appreciation for people who commit to help where they can and who involve themselves in lots of issues. These people have supported me with the callings I have felt passionate to lead on and have enabled me to pursue them. They include some of the trustees of Women Without Roofs, who have aided the charity whilst also being committed to other needs, and amazing and dedicated team members in the various anti-human-trafficking works I have set up and been involved in. I am so grateful to them. These people need and demonstrate two great gifts. Principally, they demonstrate prayerful discernment, which is required to identify the leaders and causes they support and follow. Once involved, they personify encouragement as they willingly support and serve the groups they join. Every leader needs these types of people to help them change the world and they are of great value to God too.

Secondly, across our culture there are people needed within media to highlight, uncover and bring attention to suffering and injustice. Christians who can serve faithfully and with wisdom as journalists, and in the now countless other opportunities created by social media, are necessary to our society.

Their role is to uncover and truthfully tell what others do not see, so that problems can be addressed and injustice does not remain hidden. This calling goes far beyond simply sharing and liking on social media, but instead it is about shining a light into darkness by revealing what is not known. Truth leads to justice and we find in Isaiah a description of the desperate state society falls into if truth is not made known: 'justice is driven back, and righteousness stands at a distance; truth has stumbled in the streets, honesty cannot enter. Truth is nowhere to be found, and whoever shuns evil becomes a prey. The LORD looked and was displeased that there was no justice' (Isaiah 59:14–15, NIV). Again, this role requires an interest in multiple issues, and a role in the media may be your calling if you have felt unsatisfied settling for just one subject over the past few days while working through this book.

A third arena in which Christians with multiple passions and interests are needed is politics. The number of issues a politician is expected to be acquainted with, and to vote knowledgeably about, is staggering and they range across local, national and international affairs. We are called to 'Speak up for those who cannot speak for themselves, for the rights of all who are destitute' (Proverbs 31:8, NIV) Sadly many Christians remain put off from politics as they find it difficult to identify which party to join, and there is a lack of role models to follow into this key area. Whilst it is true that no political party comes close to representing God's kingdom rule on earth, there are good points about most parties and it is possible to find Christians already involved in every mainstream party, in countless countries. Many scholars agree that both right-wing and left-wing parties represent different foci of biblical teaching about how to live and engage in society. Tim Keller[16] notes that 'what the Bible says about social justice cannot be tied to any one political system or economic policy'. Robert Putnam and David Campbell[17] agree, and foresee that 'we should expect religion and politics to align in new ways as political entrepreneurs work to construct new coalitions'. Could you be one of these political entrepreneurs, uniting people around your passion for others and your vision to transform the world?

Dear Fellow Traveller,

Even if you can not be an active member of a political party, there is a role for every Christian to play in politics.[18] I have found a home in Britain's left-wing Labour party and just weeks after joining was delighted to receive ballot forms to help select the party's European candidates. The winning candidate, who subsequently became an MEP, is now known to me. I believe that all Christians should desire to want their voice heard within politics; there is tremendous opportunity for those who get involved. In the UK, a typical party constituency group consists of 100 to 200 members and these people often get the chance to stand as local nominees and are able to vote for and choose parliamentary candidates. They have a very powerful voice on many matters and it may well be that if you are hearing a cacophony from God, politics is for you.

Go for it,

Anna

Finally, if you're finding yourself stirred about countless local issues, then a role in leading your local church may be for you. Of course not everyone is qualified to be a vicar or pastor, but it may be possible for you to become qualified, or there may be some other role for you to play in ministering to and enabling your church members to transform the world, beginning with your local area. This option is listed last because for many Christians who feel called to 'doing more', the first and only way they perceive to do this is through local church leadership. Church leaders are familiar to us and provide great role models. However, the options I have given above, media and politics, are often largely ignored and so I wanted to give them priority here.

If today has not made much sense to you, then in all likelihood you are probably being called to direct your passion to change the world at a single issue. Why not re-read yesterday's thoughts and pray through them again.

Ask yourself

Are you feeling stirred about multiple issues? Do you feel as though you are hearing a cacophony from God? Are you stirred by any of these reasons why you might be hearing this cacophony and excited about what you could do with it? Note down these feelings.

Pray

Pray that you will hear God speaking to you clearly about what He wants you to do and that you would be obedient.

Day 21: Are you a lion or a lamb?

By now my hope is that the particular issue or group of people to which you are called to transform is becoming clearer. If you have not reached this point yet, you may want to spend longer going over the last 20 days before moving on.

Once you have identified your calling with a fair degree of clarity, there is a need to define your strategy. Will you take on the world by espousing the characteristics of a lion or those of a lamb? A lion's approach is to get angry, to roar and to fight against injustice. A lamb on the other hand sacrifices everything they have for the good of others. Jesus was likened to both a lion and a lamb at different occasions in His ministry, and there is nothing to stop us, like Him, bearing both identities. Nonetheless, it is beneficial to think about both approaches and to seek God as to which one He might be particularly calling you to take on.

Lions possess two key character traits: they roar, and they are portrayed in the Bible as bold fighters. Whether we choose to enter politics or not, our mission is to 'speak up for those who can not speak up for themselves', particularly in defence of the destitute and 'for the rights of all the unfortunate' (Proverbs 31:8, NASB). These words were written to King Lemuel by his mother, though biblical scholars cannot be certain who this family were; the words are included here in Proverbs as an example of wise advice given to a king. We too are called to royal responsibilities, and these are best understood in terms of 1 Peter 2:9: 'But you are a chosen race, a royal priesthood, a holy nation, a people for God's own possession, so that you may proclaim the excellencies of Him who has called you out of darkness into His marvelous light' (NASB). If we heed this advice, then we know that we too are called to roar.

Dear Fellow Traveller,

When I realised that I should be roaring it was liberating. I had grown up in a church where to speak up against injustice was unheard of, it seemed the greatest act one could do for others was to wash up, and I hated washing up! Washing up was held up as the golden standard for anyone wanting to demonstrate they cared about others. I'm not a particularly angry person, but I do have a clear idea of what is right and wrong, as I grew older and discovered that things went on in the world that were just not right, it was hard to see how washing up was going to tackle these bigger issues. Thank God He allows us to roar!

Roarrrr!

Anna

Lions roar to communicate that the territory they are in is occupied. How appropriate for us as well. We too can roar to let Satan know that he is straying into ground that belongs to God. Doing this may take the form of lobbying, signing petitions online or taking part in a march. It might mean standing outside a high street shop informing customers of the sweatshop labour used to produce the clothes sold inside. Many Christians steer away from such activities, possibly because they fear these behaviours may be sinful, after all we are required to honour our leaders in government and authority. Yet we can be assured that 'the righteous are bold as a lion' (Proverbs 28:1, NASB) and ultimately the Lion will triumph (see Revelation 5:5 and Numbers 23).

Coupled with the notion of roaring against injustice is a prophetic role of perceiving and calling forth judgement and salvation. The lion does not just make a lot of noise, but calls others to join in the fight, and goes on to devour enemies as part of the process of bringing about justice. This is explored in the third chapter of Amos and we would do well to remember that in many cases of suffering and injustice there is an equivalent spiritual battle. We are called to fight and should not be afraid. God fights with us, and as CS Lewis famously wrote, 'He's wild, you know. Not like a tame lion'.[19]

Contained within Celtic Daily Prayer there is a stirring prayer that calls on God to enable us to roar on behalf of others. It is the Prayer of Caedmon, and these powerful lines are repeated several times within it: 'I cannot speak unless you loose my tongue; I only stammer, and I speak uncertainly; but if you touch my mouth, my Lord, then I will sing the story of your wonders!'[20] The prayer elaborates further: 'He [Jesus] said: "How dare you wrap God up in good behaviour, and tell the poor that they should be like you? How can you live at ease with riches and success, while those I love go hungry and are oppressed? It really is for such a time as this that I was given breath." His words were dangerous, not safe or tidy.' Here we see Jesus described as being angry. He is dangerous because He challenges the expected practices of His day. We are called to do likewise, and my hope is that this will be a relief to many of you reading this: we don't need to be tame.

Being a lamb is a powerful and biblical calling too. A lamb represents sacrifice and is completely countercultural to the ways of the world. In transforming the world you will almost certainly find that you have to relinquish your time, and giving money to causes is one of the best-known sacrificial ways to help others. There is also a sense of sacrifice when we pay more for goods because we choose to buy ethically made or environmentally friendly products. Romans 12:1–2 exhort us to play the role of the lamb in order to understand and bring about God's good will 'Therefore, I urge you, brothers and sisters, in view of God's mercy, to offer your bodies as a living sacrifice, holy and pleasing to God – this is your true and proper worship. Do not conform to the pattern of this world, but be transformed by the renewing of your mind. Then you will be able to test and approve what God's will is – his good, pleasing and perfect will' (NIV).

Jesus is our greatest role model for that of a lamb: He gave His life by dying a brutal death on the cross so that we are saved. He has paid the ultimate sacrifice, but we too have a worthy calling to take part in God's great plan for humankind: 'you also, like living stones, are being built into a spiritual house to be a holy priesthood, offering spiritual sacrifices acceptable to God through Jesus Christ' (1 Peter 2:5, NIV). The biblical mandate is clear – we are to be like Christ, and so sacrifice is to be expected. How much we sacrifice is harder to determine; in giving our time and money to others we can be tempted to believe that everything rests on us and that the more we give the more successful we will be at changing lives. Like Abraham, we too should remember that 'God himself will provide the lamb for the burnt offering' (Genesis 22:8, NIV).

It is unlikely that the roles of lion and lamb are entirely mutually exclusive, and this is being recognised more and more by Christian organisations. Groups such as Tearfund, Christian Aid and CAFOD, traditionally seen as merely channels for us to sacrifice money, have passionate advocacy teams that campaign for change and offer individuals many ways to get involved both as a lion and as a lamb.

Ask yourself

How appropriate is the lion or the lamb role in transforming the situation you are called to? Are there already lions or lambs addressing the situation? How could you help and complement them? Is a change of approach required?

Pray

Ask God to help you understand the roles of lion and lamb more clearly, and how they apply in the circumstances you wish to see transformed. Pray that God would help you be a lion and/or lamb to achieve His will.

Day 22: Character, skills and abilities

_____

God does not present an idea or problem to us without equipping us to solve it; He sincerely desires to use you to transform His world and will not leave you scratching your head wondering how on earth to start. In fact, He has been waiting for you and your unique set of talents to come along so He can involve you in His plans. If you feel strongly called to rectify an issue or aid a group of people then the good news is that you will already possess many of the abilities needed to solve it. In some cases you will be able to help people by yourself, in other situations it might be that you know the other people who can assist, and you are able to organise them to work together.

The Old Testament contains many lengthy passages where God reveals His plans for the Promised Land, which tribe should live where, His law for every aspect of life as God's people, His plans for the temple, what each implement should be made of and how big each should be, who should do what jobs in the temple, and what they should wear. The chapters go on and on, and if you are not familiar with them then please try reading Leviticus, Deuteronomy and Chronicles. God's attention to detail in these books is overwhelming. He knows exactly who and what is available to achieve His plans, and the skills and abilities of His people, the Israelites. He then uses these to create wealth and peace through good use of land and laws, and initiates incredible beauty in the temple.

God knows us just as well. He knows what we are good at, what we enjoy (or don't enjoy – washing up, anyone?), who we know, who we like working with and how we like to work. Psalm 139 describes how intimately God cares for us and how He knows everything about us: 'O Lord, You have searched me and known me. You know when I sit down and when I rise up; You understand my thought from afar. You scrutinize my path and my lying down, And are intimately acquainted with all my ways' (verses 1–3, NASB). The psalm continues, 'For You formed my inward parts; You wove me in my mother's womb. I will give thanks to You, for I am fearfully and wonderfully made; Wonderful are Your works, And my soul knows it very well. My frame was not hidden from You, When I was made in secret, And skillfully wrought in the depths of the earth; Your eyes have seen my unformed substance; And in Your book were all written The days that were ordained for me, When as yet there was not one of them' (verses 13–16, NASB).

Each of us is exceptional: not only do we have unique personalities and skills inherent to our nature and bestowed on us by God before we were even born, but our background, experiences and the skills we have learnt also distinguish us from others. God will not overlook these as He calls you to transform the world; He delights in us when we use them, even our hurts and hang-ups do not hold Him back from using us.

In the parable of the talents recorded in Matthew 25:14–30, three servants are entrusted with 10, 5 and 1 talents respectively whilst their master goes away for a extended period on a long journey. (In this context a talent is a unit of weight and value, it is thought to be worth 6,000 days' wages. In the parable it is used as a metaphor for a person's gifts and skills.) Two of the servants invest the money and double the amount given to them; the master is pleased with them on his return and puts them in charge of cities and greater riches. The third servant does nothing with the talent given to him and simply buries it and returns it to his master with no interest. The master is deeply dismayed and takes the single talent from him and gives it to the servant who had faithfully looked after ten talents. The third servant is thrown out of the household, and possibly the city.

This parable presents a challenge to us. Are we faithfully using our unique skills, abilities and experiences to further God's Kingdom? My belief is that the people group or cause you have identified will need exactly the talents you possess and you have received that calling precisely because you have the right skills to bring about the changes God desires to see made.

In your journal, take some time to write a long list of your talents, including your skills, experiences, past training, innate abilities, network of friends and contacts and your character strengths. What have you learnt through the difficult times you have experienced? It may be worth completing a personality profile to understand your character better: the Myers-Briggs type indicators are widely used and there are several other variations of this. Write down what you love doing, and just like the exercise that began on day 4, notice and record instances when people have told or tell you that you are good at something. English people, like me, are not the greatest at being forthcoming with compliments, so you might need to ask them to tell you what they think you are best at! If you are from another country perhaps you will be more aware of what you are good at. Begin to build a big picture of your capabilities and as you do so think about how each could be used to transform the issue you want to see changed.

Dear Fellow Traveller,

As you ponder the particular words that you identified on days 17 and 18, when you focused on your calling, think about what they require from your skill set. For instance, I identified a calling to global issues, and in order to keep up-to-date with global matters I need to be constantly learning, being curious and meeting people with whom I can question about wider topics. This plays to the pleasure I have when learning and my continued nomadic life. Similarly, as I try to tackle poverty in all its dimensions through running Women Without Roofs, I am confronted with multiple causes and possible solutions. I enjoy ideas and pondering on ethical dilemmas, so I love the work I do. You too can find this same fulfilment and sense of usefulness and purposefulness as you employ your unique talents to transform the context that God is calling you to.

You are exceptional!

Anna

Ask yourself

What are your skills, abilities, experiences and preferences? Ask others to help you identify what you are good at and what your strengths are. What do you love doing?

Pray

Thank God for your talents and ask Him to help you use them to help others.

Day 23: Mission possible

_____

By now, if you have completed the listening exercise carried out from days 4 to 17, you will have discerned who you want to help. You may also know how and what you want to transform because of the strategy thinking you have done since then. In addition, you are now aware of your God-given abilities and strengths. It is therefore time to write a mission statement incorporating all of these. It will most likely be a few sentences long and capture everything you know God is calling you to.

Dear Fellow Traveller,

I know writing a mission statement for yourself sounds a little crazy and overly ambitious but you really should have one for your life.

Really!

Anna

They provide an invaluable tool for testing new opportunities that come your way and for seeing if you are on the track God has called you to be on. If the opportunity or track match your mission statement, then go for it!

For some inspiration look up some companies and organisations that you admire and find out what their mission statements are. If you know someone who has read through this book before you and they reported that it helped them start to change the world, then ask them what their mission statement is now. Here are some mission statements that I like. I've included statements of different lengths because it really is up to you how much you want to include in your own mission statement.

People Tree: For every beautiful garment People Tree makes, there's an equally beautiful change happening somewhere in the world. When you wear People Tree, you look good and feel good knowing your unique garment was made with respect for people and the planet.

Tearfund: When a community lifts itself out of poverty, everything changes. Poverty does more than exhaust, starve, trap and kill people. It destroys their sense of worth, limits their horizons, robs people of the chance to reach their full potential. Tearfund's call is to follow Jesus where the need is greatest. We long for new life and a new sense of worth for people. We do whatever it takes to end poverty and rebuild poor communities. We work through local churches, because they're Jesus' body on earth, ready to care for the whole person – and the whole community – inside and out.

Amnesty: We are Amnesty International UK. We work to protect men, women and children wherever justice, freedom, truth and dignity are denied.

To write your own, first of all take the most meaningful keywords from days 17 and 18, when you identified the transformation you wanted to see occur in the world. If you are a mind map kind of person, write these in large letters spread out across a piece of blank paper, otherwise just list them.

Add to the piece of paper significant words that identify the skills, strengths, character traits and experiences you identified yesterday. Write each of them next to or between the areas where you prayerfully believe they apply. Draw lines and doodle as much as you like to highlight all the connections between the change you believe you are called to make happen, and the abilities you have to make it happen.

Do a sense check – have you written down everything you feel stirred about? Now bring your ideas into sentences and create your mission statement – praying as you do this. Ask yourself what it is you'd like to be known for. Don't feel obliged to include everything from your sheet of paper – use the words to draw out the key themes and identify strong impressions. Consolidate until you feel you have captured the essence of the undertaking God is calling you to.

As you reflect on your written mission statement, it should make you smile and inspire you. If it does not, then rewrite it. It is not intended to be a ball and chain that commits you to a certain way of behaving, nor a list of specific targets that you feel obliged to hit. Your mission statement should be unique to you and will be used by the Spirit to inspire and guide you, as well as help you overcome any tough times ahead.

Now write it everywhere – on bookmarks, on your mobile phone's background screen, on Post-its in your car, on social media. Look at it often and stick to it!

Ask yourself

Does the mission statement I have written clearly capture what God has been telling me over the past few weeks that He wants me to do? Does it inspire and challenge me? If not, think about rewriting it.

If you would like extra help with this process then professional help can be invaluable. Amanda Rose at Career Tree is wonderfully supportive. Find her at www.facebook.com/CareerTree1.

Pray

Ask God to help you stick to the mission He is calling you to.

Day 24: Some love with that, please

_____

The past few days have been focused on ourselves and how God wants to uniquely use us to reach others. It is easy to forget that transforming the world is about others, not ourselves, and we do it through and because of a deep love for them. 1 John 4:19 says 'We love, because He first loved us' (NASB). Pondering, therefore, on God's great love for us, and reflecting on the redeeming grace He has shown us in our own journeys, however difficult, can be a vast well of love for others on which to draw.

Dear Fellow Traveller,

When in Nepal I discovered that it has a spiritual backdrop derived from Hinduism, Buddhism and Animism. These religions say that the life we are living right now is not our only one, and that we have had past lives. How our life pans out this time around, for good or bad, and the blessings or curses we receive, are due to our actions in this and in previous lives. This concept is known as 'karma' – it means that if we suffer in this life it is because of previous wrong-doing and we are to blame for what happens to us. If we do not want to experience suffering in a subsequent life we need to overcome and bear our sufferings in this life and remain faithful to the gods throughout. A tragic corollary of this is that if someone helps you to overcome your suffering, they are in effect not allowing you to bear the burden that you should be, according to karma. Therefore you may find your situation no better in your next life because you still haven't paid the price for previous wrongdoing, even if that was several lives ago.

This is a terrible lie and results in little or no help being given to the poor, and no love shown towards them. The rich are free to pursue their own ends and have permission to ignore and overlook the needy. The implications are not limited to individuals and families but the whole of society is infected; entire people groups are kept down and subordinated. How different to the Christian faith, that encourages care for the needy and a selfless life of love and service in adoration of a loving God!

Humbly,

Anna

The above example is included because it can be useful to understand what both God's and our love for people is not like; it can be helpful to remind ourselves that there are different responses to poverty and suffering and how they contrast starkly with Christian love. Thinking more deeply about God's love, Psalm 107 provides a valuable model for reflecting on our own journeys and for identifying different aspects of God's character that invokes love for Him and others. The words are beautiful, let them soak into you and remind you of what God has accomplished in your life, how He has overcome your brokenness.

His love is committed, unchanging and lovingly determined: 'Give thanks to the LORD, for he is good; his love endures forever. Let the redeemed of the LORD tell their story – those he redeemed from the hand of the foe, those he gathered from the lands, from east and west, from north and south' (verses 1–3, NIV).

God's love brings us home: 'Some wandered in desert wastelands, finding no way to a city where they could settle. They were hungry and thirsty, and their lives ebbed away. Then they cried out to the LORD in their trouble, and he delivered them from their distress. He led them by a straight way to a city where they could settle. Let them give thanks to the LORD for his unfailing love and his wonderful deeds for mankind, for he satisfies the thirsty and fills the hungry with good things' (verses 4–9, NIV).

The love of the Lord grants us freedom: 'Some sat in darkness, in utter darkness, prisoners suffering in iron chains, because they rebelled against God's commands and despised the plans of the Most High. So he subjected them to bitter labour; they stumbled, and there was no one to help. Then they cried to the LORD in their trouble, and he saved them from their distress. He brought them out of darkness, the utter darkness, and broke away their chains. Let them give thanks to the LORD for his unfailing love and his wonderful deeds for mankind, for he breaks down gates of bronze and cuts through bars of iron' (verses 10–16, NIV).

His love makes us whole: 'Some became fools through their rebellious ways and suffered affliction because of their iniquities. They loathed all food and drew near the gates of death. Then they cried to the LORD in their trouble, and he saved them from their distress. He sent out his word and healed them; he rescued them from the grave. Let them give thanks to the LORD for his unfailing love and his wonderful deeds for mankind. Let them sacrifice thank-offerings and tell of his works with songs of joy' (verses 17–22, NIV).

God's love brings peace in every situation, no matter how stormy: 'Some went out on the sea in ships; they were merchants on the mighty waters. They saw the works of the LORD, his wonderful deeds in the deep. For he spoke and stirred up a tempest that lifted high the waves. They mounted up to the heavens and went down to the depths; in their peril their courage melted away. They reeled and staggered like drunkards; they were at their wits' end. Then they cried out to the LORD in their trouble, and he brought them out of their distress. He stilled the storm to a whisper; the waves of the sea were hushed. They were glad when it grew calm, and he guided them to their desired haven. Let them give thanks to the LORD for his unfailing love and his wonderful deeds for mankind. Let them exalt him in the assembly of the people and praise him in the council of the elders' (verses 23–32, NIV).

God's deeds demonstrate His loving care for us: 'He turned rivers into a desert, flowing springs into thirsty ground, and fruitful land into a salt waste, because of the wickedness of those who lived there. He turned the desert into pools of water and the parched ground into flowing springs; there he brought the hungry to live, and they founded a city where they could settle. They sowed fields and planted vineyards that yielded a fruitful harvest; he blessed them, and their numbers greatly increased, and he did not let their herds diminish. Then their numbers decreased, and they were humbled by oppression, calamity and sorrow; he who pours contempt on nobles made them wander in a trackless waste. But he lifted the needy out of their affliction and increased their families like flocks. The upright see and rejoice, but all the wicked shut their mouths. Let the one who is wise heed these things and ponder the loving deeds of the LORD' (verses 33–43, NIV).

I can not help but be reminded of what God has done in my own life when I read this psalm. He has truly done amazing things and without Him I would be nothing. Yet our love towards Him should not only be motivated by gratitude. Of course it is right and natural to be thankful but our love should go beyond that to a deep adoration and worship of His character. We should love Him for who He is, not only for what He has done. Imagine if your children or spouse loved you only for the things you provided for them. That kind of love falls far short of the love you want them to express towards you, where to be together in each other's company is far better than anything you could give them.

Ask yourself

Are you familiar with God's love for you? Does it help you to love others more with the same kind of love? What does God's love and working in your own life reveal to you about His character?

Pray

Ask God to reveal to you more and more of His great love for all humankind and the different ways that it works. Pray that you would be able to love others with the same type of love that He does, and that like His love, it would endure.

AND ACTION!

It is time to use your God-given passion to see the world transformed. Get involved and go!

Day 25: The rubber hits the road

Maybe you are already involved with a group of people trying to change the world for the better, or maybe you have never done anything like this before. However, it is time to dedicate yourself to God's goals, to take all that love and passion you have for others and to put it into action. You will prove that you have been on internal journey, better getting to know God's will for you, by your actions. Matthew 11:19 says 'wisdom is proved right by her deeds' (NIV) and James concurs 'In the same way, faith by itself, if it is not accompanied by action, is dead' (James 2:17, NIV).

First off, Peter tells us how to get ready for action: 'prepare your minds for action, keep sober in spirit, fix your hope completely on the grace to be brought to you at the revelation of Jesus Christ' (1 Peter 1:13, NASB).

Dear Fellow Traveller,

Keep your mission statement before you – memorising it is helpful and it should be a hopeful expression of what you want to achieve. Also keep in mind your greater understanding of who and how God has called you to transform the world, from days 17 and 18. Now step into all that God has planned for you – this stage is exciting!

Wow!

Anna

If you are not already involved with the group you wish to work alongside, the first step is to make contact. You need to let them know you are passionate about their cause and want to help change their situation. At this stage your task is to learn as much as you can: to see what is already being done about the problem, and to understand how your passion fits with it. Visit the group if you can and ask as many questions as possible – taking an interest is an encouragement in itself to those already involved in the work. If there is no one local to you already doing something, much of this work will need to take place over the internet.

As you take a look at what is being done, try to work out, through observation and asking, what end point they are working towards. For instance, a homeless charity can help in many ways: they may simply be trying to help homeless people get through the night, through providing food and shelter; they may have a long-term programme to help the destitute contribute to society by finding work for them; or their end goal may be to holistically restore them in mind, body and spirit. Identifying common end goals between groups and your own mission and calling could very well be more important than who a particular group helps.

When making your first approach to a group and offering to get involved, you may well be asked to do something that does not match your mission statement or calling. Think carefully about turning them down: right now your task is to learn and you could help them for a short while. Meeting their needs is a sure way to demonstrate your commitment to the issue. This could be a step in the door that that will later offer further opportunities that fit more closely with what you understand your calling to be. Sometimes, however, you may need to turn down a request for help, knowing it is not what God is calling you to do. Pray for wisdom as you do this and heed Micah's call to act justly: 'He has shown you, O mortal, what is good. And what does the LORD require of you? To act justly and to love mercy and to walk humbly with your God' (Micah 6:8, NIV).

If you are already involved in working with a group of people that God has clearly called you to transform through this book, then you have a great starting point. He may be asking you to do something new or different however. Cautiously, and with much prayer, consider the options open to you. Should you be taking on greater responsibilities, or are there different approaches that God is calling you to take? Let others know of your renewed commitment to the people and cause.

As you start to take action there is great pleasure to be had in meeting new people, being curious about what they are doing and involving yourself without any pressure. Enjoy these first steps into God's plan for your life, they may set the direction for the rest of your time on earth, and the opportunities before you have potential to hugely bless you and others.

Ask yourself

Who can you contact right now by ringing, emailing or visiting so that you are acting on God's calling in your life?

Pray

As you make contact, pray that you get involved in the right areas and quickly feel assurance that you are doing God's will. Pray that love will sustain you and you will not become distracted. Enjoy the pleasure of meeting new people and being curious about how they are transforming the world.

Day 26: Doing godly research

If you haven't noticed already, not everyone agrees with each other and on entering the realm of helping others, the right course of action is often contentious or unclear. Rarely does a solution to a problem fit all similar problems and seldom do people agree what the best solution is. Understanding all these points of view and opinions is vital, not only so that you can achieve the best and most godly transformation of a situation, but also so that you can win people over to joining with you to change the world.

Take the issue of poverty, a well-known concept and one most people would agree means a lack of material wealth. Yet solving poverty is difficult, and if it were easy to remove global poverty, it would have been done by now. Even sending a man to the moon must be easier because it has already been achieved.

Dear Fellow Traveller,

I have an MSc in Poverty Reduction and spent a whole week of the course reading and debating what poverty is, and another full week analysing what development is. Those who are not poor commonly define poverty as a lack of material possessions, but those who are classed as impoverished list a host of other factors that for them define poverty before they identify lack of wealth as a problem. Higher on their list of priorities are more indefinite standards, each being much harder to measure than simply looking at a bank balance (or counting the cash in a jar).

Poverty, as defined by participants in a poverty relief programme in Rwanda[21]:

1. *Poverty is an empty heart.*
2. *Not knowing your abilities and strengths.*
3. *Not being able to make progress.*
4. *Isolation.*
5. *No hope or belief in yourself. Knowing you can't take care of your family.*

6. *Broken relationships.*
7. *Not knowing God.*
8. *Not having basic things to eat. Not having money.*
9. *Poverty is a consequence of not sharing.*
10. *Lack of good thoughts.*

If this wasn't confusing enough, when we start to think about the solutions to poverty, as defined by the list, it can seem even harder to know where to start.

Confused,

Anna

Typical church solutions often start with charity and meet immediate needs of the impoverished, such as operating a food bank, whereby food to last three or four days is provided to those in need. Right-wing politicians believe a vibrant economy will create jobs for all and the wealth of the rich will 'trickle down'[22] to the poor; they advocate removing trade barriers so that impoverished nations can participate in the global market for goods and services. Left-wing politicians will more likely champion the role of the state in providing safety nets, such as unemployment benefit and overseas aid, so that those without work can still have an income to support their family. Non-government organisations will call on governments to protect the rights of the poor to education and safe housing, and others will organise community micro-saving and credit schemes in developing countries to build social and financial capital amongst the poor.[23]

My point in listing all these different views is that the method you hope to use to help the people you believe God is calling you to may be erroneous, or, though correct, may not be sufficient on its own and will fail to solve a complex, deep-seated problem. Many views and solutions might be needed, therefore it is vital that you conduct research into what works. This need not only be reading textbooks – instead, how about speaking to experts, watching TED talks online, and visiting other groups working with similar people? If you are passionate about a cause, it will be a joy to learn about it.

Your research should include three broad areas: biblical, secular and first-hand. Taking a topical tough subject and plumbing the depths of the Bible to seek out answers is a great way to gain wisdom and is also a very good method for increasing your biblical literacy. There is a spiritual realm behind many issues and understanding and overcoming it is key to the success of any project hoping to transform the world.

Secular research is necessary because it is there that you will find data and analysis that dissect different problems in order to fully comprehend them.[24] The secular field contains a great amount of creative thinking about problems and rigorous academic research is a treasure trove of information and ideas.

You may neither have the time nor inclination to undertake a degree in the particular issue that stirs your heart, but it is possible to read suggested books on topics and many academics now write popular books on subjects they usually teach on.[25] Furthermore, researching across cultures and countries is often enlightening and may prove extremely valuable to the work you wish to do. Your country will certainly not have all the answers to the problems it faces and much can be learnt from how other cultures tackle those same issues. Even novels can play a significant role in understanding the cultural history of the people you hope to assist.[26]

Speaking to face-to-face with those you wish to help and the people already aiding them is also incredibly valuable. You may think you know their problem and how to solve it, but they may tell you something completely different! The Cinnamon Network[27] connects church groups to one another and even provides a franchise-type model for social action projects. Through them you can meet people doing similar things to you and learn from their mistakes and achievements.

Doing research is included in the Action section of this book because it should be carried out continuously – it is not just done once, a plan made, and then that is it. For many, research may also be the only action they can take right now, particularly if they have young children or others to care for. It is an action in its own right. Remember, though, the cautionary words from day 11: the purpose of carrying out research is not to become bloated on knowledge, but to increase our wisdom.

Ask yourself

What do you need to understand more about in order to successfully help and intervene in the issue you care for? Can you order a book, watch a video online or arrange to speak to someone now so that you are on the path to gaining wisdom?

Pray

Ask God to direct you to pieces of research that will help you learn how to achieve His goals. Pray that He will give you wisdom to understand and apply what you learn.

Day 27: Learning on the job

So, you have started on your journey and taken a step of faith by meeting up with some people involved in the issue you know God has spoken to you about. How did that initial meeting go? If you are anything like me, you will have made mistakes already; perhaps you spoke down to someone you wanted to value. Maybe you nervously made a joke that did not go down too well or if you are conducting research perhaps you have already wasted heaps of money on books, but have missed the chance to speak to someone directly about your cause. It is alright, we all make mistakes and they are often a brilliant chance to learn and reflect. Keep writing your journal as you record and contemplate on what happens as you get involved. This should be carried out actively, not passive as an afterthought, hence the reason for including it in this section.

Proverbs 11:2 (NIV) reminds us that 'When pride comes, then comes disgrace, but with humility comes wisdom'. We could all do with a dose of humility.

Dear Fellow Traveller,

Through running Women Without Roofs in Nepal we have certainly got things wrong many times. In 2010 a new family – a woman and her three children – were referred to us for help by their pastor. The daughters were nine and eleven and their brother was just two. These girls were not in school so we immediately enrolled them in the local primary, with lofty aims of breaking the cycle of poverty through education. What we failed to take into account was the tinge of grey in the girls' hair: they were desperately malnourished and couldn't possibly concentrate in school. It was a disastrous start to their school careers as most days they were told off for not paying attention in class. The girls also worked on alternate days for another family in exchange for food, in fact that may have been the only food they were receiving at the time, and so us enrolling them in school took them away from work as well.

After a while we reviewed the whole family's situation and began providing nutritional supplements to them as well as oil to stir into their rice – one of the biggest problems was a lack of fat in their diet. No matter how much plain boiled rice they ate, nutritionally it was simply insufficient. In 2011 we opened a women's home and this family were one of the first to move in. The mother began cooking all the meals for the women in the home and it is wonderful to see her now give to others and provide for them out of the plenty in the kitchen. Their lives have been changed beyond recognition and just last year the girls won an academic competition at school. God was so gracious throughout the whole situation and enabled us to undo our mistakes and learn from them. I am grateful for our staff in Nepal who remained flexible and generous throughout.

Often wrong,

Anna

More broadly speaking as we have attempted to overcome the poverty of women in Nepal we have discovered that it is not just a monetary problem. Other factors, such as caste, education, health (including mental health), safety, religion and social disorder play significant roles too. We simply try to do what we can, with cautious optimism that we will find a solution that suits each woman's particular situation. Where we don't have expertise, particularly in the case of mental health, we have found partners[28] to help us.

As Christians we get it wrong a lot and we should not expect to get everything right just because we call Jesus our saviour. In the past there were Christians in favour of slavery, before that Christians murdered over 100,000 people across the Middle East in the crusades. Today right-wing Christians in the US argue in favour of gun rights and remain quiet on subjects such as wealth inequality. Pride and selfishness twist not only our actions but our beliefs too and we need to be aware of our own wrongfulness.

Proceeding with humility then, and with willingness to learning as you do it, is paramount. In the business world this might be called continuous improvement. Do not, however, be cautious in regards to your calling: if God has spoken clearly to you about who He wishes you to help then boldly cling on to that hopeful vision. Do not compromise on who you are called to, but be humble about how you help them. As we remain committed to our God-given mandate, the Holy Spirit will teach us. 1 John 2:27 (NIV) confirms: 'as his anointing teaches you about all things and as that anointing is real, not counterfeit – just as it has taught you, remain in him'. It seems our role is to remain in Him, close to Him: there will be constant choices in our work to transform the world, but we need only to listen to Him and to remain. When faced with baffling choices, do not worry. Peter reminds us that humility helps us to remain close to God: 'Humble yourselves, therefore, under God's mighty hand, that he may lift you up in due time. Cast all your anxiety on him because he cares for you' (1 Peter 5:6–7, NIV).

Ask yourself

How has your helping to transform gone so far? What mistakes have you made? Are there any areas in which you are prone to arrogance and in which you believe you know the answers rather than seeking God for them?

Pray

Ask God to grant you humility to learn from your mistakes and to let Him teach you.

Day 28: Being a good consumer

One of the most practical and influential ways that everybody can help to change the world is by exercising their power as a consumer. Many people complain about politicians and lament that in general they are only able to vote for their representative in government every four to five years. When it comes to shopping though, every purchase we make is a vote for the company and the product. This adds up to a lot of votes and companies pay vast amounts to identify, analyse and predict consumer purchasing trends. No matter who you are called to help, there will almost certainly be ways you can use consumer power to help them; whether it be supporting women in Africa through buying jewellery from Created by Tearfund, or helping the mentally ill where you live by purchasing upcycled furniture from MIND. Your purchasing muscle can be used to provide good working conditions for many people and offer them a dignified means of providing for themselves and their families. Money does not make the world go round, but it can certainly be used as a means of cheering on those doing good in the world.

Dear Fellow Traveller,

Being a good consumer can empower you and others – to me it feels good to pass by the non-fair-trade bananas and buy the fairly produced ones instead. I get to stick a metaphorical finger up at sellers who don't care about their workers. There are heaps of websites, books and publications that give listings of fair trade products and where to buy them, take a look at the Fairtrade Foundation's website[29], on it you'll find over 4,500 products listed. There are some critics of fair trade labelling, who argue that once a product qualifies to use the Fairtrade symbol on its packaging, there are no checks to ensure the company maintains its fair trade operating principles. But a Fairtrade symbol is still better than none and if you are worried about whether a product is really fairly traded there are plenty of resources online.[30][31]

Empowered,

Anna

It can be demanding on your wallet if you decide to buy everything from fair trade suppliers, including clothing, and to purchase environmentally friendly products as well as donating money to charity, etc. The costs soon mount up, but if your budget is limited I urge you to focus on buying products that give integrity to you and match the people and cause you feel God is calling you to. For instance if you want to work against human trafficking, then make sure you are buying fair trade chocolate. Be unrelenting on the particular causes close to your heart, as your house fills with 'good' products and you give gifts (ie a box of fair trade chocolates) to others that meet your criteria you'll be a great witness to them about the issue close to your heart and it may lead to them getting involved in what you are up to. Sending out mixed messages, ie buying the cheap, non-fair-trade chocolate but telling everyone you care about stopping human trafficking, only compromises you. This is particularly true in the UK where there is a vast range of fair trade products available. The choice not to buy fair trade in the UK is an active decision, not something forced upon consumers.

Another way to look at the increased cost of buying 'good' products from fair and honest suppliers is that it works like a tariff on your lifestyle. You will have less to spend and will in turn buy less, but this will help you 'reduce, reuse and recycle'. The additional costs act as an additional spur to buy less and look after what you do have. A lifestyle conducted like this is not easy, but that does not mean it should not be an option for some, think of it as a form of simplifying your life in the manner of monasticism.

We are not only consumers on an individual basis, but the countries we live in also engage in global trade and that is where the role of trade justice fits in. As the Trade Justice movement describes it, their aim is to 'Make world trade work for people and the planet'.[32] There are many organisations that argue for fair trading rules between countries so that workers in those countries are not exploited and have opportunity to flourish through meaningful employment.[33] Through organisations such as Global Justice Now[34] it is possible to join them in lobbying government for fairer trading rules and for more power to go to the poor, particularly the poor in the Global South. In 2015 they were actively involved in opposing the Transatlantic Trade and Investment Partnership that would have undermined public services and democracy in the UK. For instance corporations would be permitted to sue governments if they acted in a way that damaged profits, ie by imposing environmental safeguards.

Buying from certain countries may not only empower and provide for the workers, but also empowers and recognises the country itself. This is true when purchasing Palestinian Olive Oil,[35] which the Daily Telegraph has declared the most ethical product ever produced. Similarly, buying raisins from Afghanistan helps that country to switch from growing poppies for opium to a far healthier industry with not nearly so many nasty offshoots in the form of drug and people trafficking.

Taking action on causes close to your heart need not be any harder than taking more time to consider what you are buying at your supermarket. As consumers we are powerful, and as we are encouraged in

Proverbs 31, our interaction with the marketplace and how we spend our money matters to God and marks us out as worthy.

Ask yourself

What items should I boycott or prioritise buying so that I am not compromising my calling? What could I switch to buying from today so that my money is cheering on those doing good in the world?

Pray

Pray for the strength to stick to your buying goals and the opportunity to tell others why you have chosen to buy and shop from the producers you have chosen.

Day 29: Keep on turning up

We can make changing the world so complicated, but very often it is just about being there, about showing up, and making a difference through our very presence. Keep going with your commitment to a people group or cause and if you stick at it you will make changes whether you perceive them or not.

You will be tempted to give up on your cause. Satan is real and he has no desire to see people freed from whatever is oppressing them. You will almost certainly have thoughts – part of spiritual opposition – along the lines that you are not helping at all, that the issue is too complicated for you to solve, and that you are creating other problems. The temptation to give up will be strong. You may also suffer physical symptoms that make you want to turn away. Tiredness causes a lot of people to give up – of course some tiredness is genuine, but it is astonishing how Satan uses tiredness to turn people away from their calling. Likewise busyness and lack of resources also get in the way. Keep close to God in prayer to discern if those are genuine reasons for not doing something.

Dear Fellow Traveller,

Keep a simple commitment to your cause – even if just means spending half an hour with someone each week, or reading a book a month.

Stick at it,

Anna

Even if you don't feel your getting involved is making a positive difference it may well be that simply by being present you prevent difficult situations from happening and a quiet word here and there, spoken with wisdom, can have big impact. This biblical adage reminds us of the power of our words and our tongue in particular '...take ships as an example. Although they are so large and are driven by strong winds, they are steered by a very small rudder wherever the pilot wants to go' (James 3:4, NIV). As you begin to make a regular commitment to a group or cause you will become integrated with others and it is important to keep committing yourself to God and to the group. Wherever you go, you take Christ and the Holy Spirit – you can trust Him to use you for good, but He can only do that if you turn up.

Actions add up with those of others too. Yesterday we discussed buying fair trade products – it is very unlikely that your purchases alone will be enough to sustain a fair trade supplier (I'm trying with chocolate!) but if others can be persuaded to buy from them too, then their business will be sustainable. In 2015, while living in the USA it is interesting to observe the cultural differences between Americans and Europeans. I have noticed that Americans, in the area in which I live, do not seem to believe, or act, as if their actions will add up. Fair trade products are difficult to find and Americans' strong sense of individuality and self-autonomy mean that many of them oppose curbs on their freedom to choose how they live. For instance, measures to reduce their carbon footprint are viewed as unwelcome controlling from government.[36] That is not to say Europeans behave perfectly – we have a tendency to view our choices as sacrifices and we martyr ourselves rather than see the opportunities before us as chances to change the world for the better. There are more Americans who have seized on the business potential in recycling and reusing and have made millions from setting up companies to do so.[37]

David knew the value of turning up and getting involved, after all he volunteered to fight Goliath because he knew that God was on the Israelites' side. He wrote these beautiful words that inspire us to stick at what we're called to too (Goliath slaying not compulsory!): 'Trust in the Lord and do good; Dwell in the land and cultivate faithfulness. Delight yourself in the LORD; and He will give you the desires of your heart. Commit your way to the LORD, trust also in Him, and He will do it. He will bring forth your righteousness as the light and your judgment as the noonday' (Psalm 37:3–6, NASB). There are six instructions in these verses for us, namely we should trust, do good, dwell, cultivate faithfulness, delight and commit. Each of these is appropriate for describing the approach we need to foster towards the causes and groups we want to see transformed.

Once you have committed yourself and if you want to do more than just turn up, then when God says you are ready you can run the race marked out for you. Hebrews 12 exhorts us to '...throw off everything that hinders and the sin that so easily entangles. And let us run with perseverance the race marked out for us, fixing our eyes on Jesus, the pioneer and perfecter of faith' (verses 1–2, NIV).

On your marks. Get set. Go!

Ask yourself

Are you ready to fully commit yourself to the issue God has called you to address? Have you noticed common obstacles to becoming more involved, such as tiredness and busyness? Are these genuine hindrances or do you need ask God to help you overcome them?

Pray

Ask God to give you the self-discipline to remain committed to the group you are involved with. Pray through the six instructions in Psalm 37 and ask God to help you follow them in your situation. Ask Him for running shoes.

Day 30: Finding role models

_____

Has anyone ever told you that they know someone you simply must meet? Or have you had that wonderful feeling, on spending time with someone, that you feel so inspired by them and have such a strong connection with them because they want to see the same transformation in the world that you do? Those are special feelings, and God uses relationships like this as a primary way to build us up. Role models inspire us and help us to see how changing the world might just be possible; they also provide useful examples of how they achieve what they do. If you're a new mum maybe you can find another mum to copy, and see how she juggles her family life with changing the world.

As you read this, you may already know who your role model is. If you don't, then a great place to start is by asking your pastor if he or she can recommend someone to you who is already transforming the world, and might have time to mentor you. Make sure you choose someone that many other people speak well of, it is dangerous to choose someone whom you think is fantastic, but has a poor reputation with others.

When you are with your role model then spend time asking lots of questions, really seek out from them how they sustain what they do, what motivates them and quiz them about the lessons they have learnt along the way. If you have hurts that you are still overcoming and have some baggage, then attempt to find someone who has surmounted similar issues, they can lead you on the safe path of overcoming, but do be careful that your time together does not drag them backwards. Meeting together with a third person may be helpful to achieve this.

Dear Fellow Traveller,

When we lived in Nepal I was approached by a woman named Eileen[38] who at the time was 80 years old. She had lived in Nepal for 50 years and was currently supporting about ten women with her own funds to pay their rent and medical bills. She was worried about what would happen to these ten women when she died and having prayed to God she was told someone from the British Camp (where I lived) would help. This was the beginning of Women Without Roofs and since that time in 2005, the charity has grown both in numbers and scope. Eileen is *still alive, though has suffer from dementia since shortly after transferring responsibility for the women to me and WWR. She is an amazing, godly woman and when I am with her I can sense the great anointing on her to minister to the people of Nepal. One of the regrets I have, however, is that I did not ask her to pray for me. Though we have prayed together many times for the women and for Nepal more generally, I never asked her to lay hands on me. I would love for some of her anointing to pass on to me, so I urge you to ask your mentors and role models to pray for you – they best know what skills and spiritual gifts you will need to succeed in your mission. In the Bible we see how Paul and Timothy had a wonderful mentoring relationship, and in the Old Testament we see that Elisha was far savvier than me – he remembered to ask for Elijah's anointing (2 Kings 2:9).*

Pray for me,

Anna

Role models need not only be people that you know, they may be people that you only read about and can be people from the past as well. Here are some eclectic ideas for role models:

Aung San Suu Kyi has maintained a peaceful struggle for democracy and human rights in Burma since the 1980s and was awarded the Nobel Peace Prize in 1991. Aung San Suu Kyi's ability to affect people and repressive regimes reflects not only her personal charisma and courage but also her devotion to democracy.

Catherine Booth was co-founder of the Salvation Army with her husband William. She was firmly committed to God, to social activism, to revival and some suggest an early feminist too; a groundbreaker in many ways.

Elizabeth Fry is a favourite. In the early 1800s she campaigned relentlessly for prison reform and set up women's groups to take care of prison children and female prisoners. She was utterly tireless and a wonderful example of someone who could relate to everybody, from prostitutes in prison to royalty. She also achieved all this and raised a family at the same time.

Heidi Baker lives in Mozambique today and with her husband Rolland founded IRIS ministries to minister to street children, since 1980 it has touched the lives of all kinds of people. Her work continues to expand across countries and she has written numerous books about the miracles she has experienced.

John Wesley was founding father of the Methodists and is known for his phenomenal preaching that led to revival both in the UK and USA, despite intense persecution.

Mahatma Gandhi is the prime model for active nonviolent resistance, which propelled the Indian struggle for independence and countless other nonviolent struggles of the twentieth century.

Martin Luther King also followed the active non-violent resistance model that Gandhi pioneered and was a preacher. King was devoted to achieving racial equality in the USA and inspired many with his dream that one day it would become reality.

Mother Teresa is also known as the Saint of Calcutta as she lived there for many years ministering to the destitute and dying. Her simple yet earnest devotion to God and the poor led to deep sacrifice and is a challenge to us all.

Nelson Mandela engaged in resistance against South Africa's ruling National Party's apartheid policies. He was imprisoned for over 20 years, yet on his release in 1990 won the Nobel Peace Prize and was inaugurated as the first democratically elected president of South Africa in 1994.

Pope Francis is the current Pope of the Catholic Church. Though history has yet to determine what his greatest legacy will be, he is already famed for his humility, his concern for the poor, and his commitment to dialogue as a way to build bridges between people of all backgrounds, beliefs, and faiths.

Shane Claiborne is a Christian 'jack of all trades' and is founder of The Simple Way, a faith community in inner-city Philadelphia that has helped to birth and connect radical faith communities around the world. He has worked with Mother Teresa, sought to bring about peace in Iraq and has a strong message for the church in America.

Steve Chalke challenges the way we Christians see things and how we respond to the world around us. He is a minister in London and founder of the Oasis Trust, a social action organisation and Stop The Traffik, a global network of activists united against human trafficking.

William Wilberforce, an evangelical Christian and a member of Parliament, who in the face of great obstacles fought for the abolition of the African slave trade and against slavery itself until they were both illegal in the British Empire. He was God-centred and his faith and writings have inspired a great many.

You. Don't forget that as you start to transform the world, you too will become a role model to those in your church and beyond. Take this responsibility seriously, the world can't be changed alone and inspiring others to get involved is a great privilege and opportunity. There will be a further look at this on day 38.

Finally, Jesus is our ultimate example of how to live and act. He is our hero, and unlike any other role model He works in and through us to transform us ever more into His likeness. No other mentor will ever want to spend as much time with us as He does. If we crave His presence and knowing more of Him, He will satisfy those longings.

Ask yourself

Who inspires you? Who would like to be more like? What is it about them that inspires you and attracts you to be like them? List those qualities. Make arrangements to meet with a role model now, or meet with or email your pastor if you need to ask them to suggest someone to you. Read a book written by or about one of the people listed above.

Pray

Ask God to help you meet and learn from a good, godly role model. Ask God to keep on changing you and for Him to give you the qualities you need to change the world.

Day 31: Team player, copycat or apostle?

Have you ever noticed that people can solve the same problems in different ways? Humans are beautifully diverse and no two people respond in exactly the same way to any given situation. When we work together to change the world, a small group of people can create endless possible solutions and benefits. Creativity is God-given and nurturing it in each other is helpful to us, good for them and does wonders for the issue we are seeking to transform. Determining your role in a team, however, takes time and practice and an acute sensitivity to God's leading and inspiration.

As you consider the best way to reach the group on your mind and transform their situation for the better, you may even now know a team of people, or an individual, who are already ministering to the group. By all means join this team and find out what they are doing and how you can help. Supporting them in their calling may be the very best way to add weight to their actions and help greater transformation come about.

Team players are vitally important in every initiative, and many famous leaders would be nowhere without the support and consistency of team players, collaborators and supporters who are often uncelebrated but critical to their success. Simply committing to turning up and getting involved, as detailed on day 29, will accomplish great change.

Dear Fellow Traveller,

I have had the privilege of leading some wonderful teams in recent years. In Nepal, Women Without Roofs employs a committed team who care deeply for the ladies we support; their greatest strength is their love for Nepal's women and they do not give up seeking to make their lives better. In the UK, the group of trustees I lead always offers good advice and are likewise committed to Nepal.

While I was living in Aldershot a group of us formed TOAST (Team Operating Against Slave Trafficking), and this team was especially wonderful to work with: they were up for anything, committed to the cause, and always positive. TOAST included a number of non-Christians, and it was the perfect vehicle for us Christians to show our love for each other and our commitment to justice and Christ. Christian team work is a powerful witness.

Together with you,

Anna

All of us bring baggage to the teams we join and each of us has weaknesses. Christ-centred teamwork allows the baggage to be shared and our hurts and weaknesses to be restored by each other. Not only do we have the privilege of addressing our cause and helping others, but we benefit from having our needs met and wounds healed by one another.

It is more than likely that God will have placed a group or cause on your heart that is not currently being addressed by anyone you know of. God sees the unseen; He knows where help is needed most and naturally this will be in areas that are currently being neglected. If this is the case for the issue you hope to address, then you will need to set up a new group or initiative where you are. The best way to go about doing this is to copy the work of a group doing similar things elsewhere and to draw on the experiences of any role models you have identified. You may only have the chance to read about their work, but if possible do try to visit them so that you can learn as much from them as possible. The Cinnamon Network (who I mentioned on day 26) can facilitate this, and they offer a franchise model for numerous ministries.

As King Solomon, the writer of Ecclesiastes observes, 'there is nothing new under the sun' (1:9, NIV) and we can know that any problems we are encountering have been addressed and overcome before. Copying solutions to issues is not cheating but demonstrates wisdom and is biblically commanded. Paul urges the Corinthians to imitate his life in Christ (1 Corinthians 4:16); in his letter to the Ephesians he tells them to follow God's example and walk in the way of love (Ephesians 5:1–2). The writer of Hebrews similarly warns the reader not to be sluggish 'but to imitate those who through faith and patience inherit what has been promised' (6:12, NIV) and furthermore to 'Remember your leaders, who spoke the word of God to you. Consider the outcome of their way of life and imitate their faith' (13:7, NIV). Successfully copying the work done by another group or person is without doubt a sure way to guarantee some success in addressing the need God has called you to meet, however, do be careful that the solution you copy is completely appropriate for the situation you find yourself in. For instance, tackling the issue of homelessness in one area might mean starting a job club, whereas in another it might mean addressing drug addiction. Keep listening to God and ask Him to help you identify what to copy and what you shouldn't.

Finally there are those rare times when God calls for something completely new to be done. In the church someone who is called to take the gospel to somewhere new may be called an apostle. They will uniquely be a gifted teacher, pastor, prophet and evangelist and will spearhead a new work of God's church (1 Corinthians 12:29, Ephesians 4:11). Apostles do not usually self-identify, but are called out and recognised by the wider church body who see and confirm the anointing upon them. In the secular world someone like an apostle would be called an entrepreneur: very often they will have great ability in all areas of a business – human resources, accounting, marketing and sales – but are exceptionally gifted in setting a vision and creating a new way of doing business. A development of this idea into the social realm has led to the introduction of a new term: a social entrepreneur. This is a person who comes up with innovative solutions to society's most pressing social problems and achieves wide-scale, societal-level change.

You may or may not be called to be an apostle, but it is possible that a new ministry you set up could be defined as apostolic, meaning it breaks new ground for the Kingdom of God. The greatest insight we have into the mind of an apostle and apostolic ministry is through Paul in the New Testament. He is firmly committed to taking the gospel to new places and clearly knows that is his calling (2 Corinthians 10:15–16). Paul's new apostolic message was that Christ had not only died for the Jews but for the Gentiles too (Ephesians 3). At the time this was completely radical, and as you are reading this you may also feel a great excitement for undertaking a radical apostolic ministry for God. That is truly wonderful – there are so many dark places that need a godly adventurer to minister there – but we see from Paul's example it was not all excitement and trailblazing. He spent a great amount of effort justifying his work and ministry in his letters and encountered opposition for being so uncompromising (Galatians 2).

If the transformational work you are being called to appears to be apostolic, then just like Paul, there are two things you need to do. First seek God relentlessly: He will be your treasure and pleasure as you advance the Kingdom. Second, ask for the support of the church and be responsive to their concerns, keeping yourself in good repute with them, just as Paul did, so that they can undergird your work. Apostles rarely work entirely alone – they often take the people of God with them into new places.

Whether you are a team player, copycat or apostle, your calling is unique and God has an important role for you to play in changing the world. Relish it and keep close to Him so that He can bless your work.

Ask yourself

How could the teams you are part of better heal the hurts of its members? Can you identify any groups to copy and learn from so that you are better prepared to transform the world? Do you recognise the excitement of being an apostle as described by Paul? Is any of the opposition he faced familiar to you too? Identify someone you could pray with about this.

Pray

Ask God to help the teams you are part of to be healthy and healing communities, where not only those that are in the group you are ministering to are healed, but where the team members are healed as well. Pray for Godly examples you can copy. Tell God you want to relentlessly pursue Him, pray for the Kingdom of God to expand into dark places.

Day 32: What is the message?

_____

By now I hope that you are burning with love and passion for a cause or people and have found a way of getting involved with trying to help them. What is your message to them, though, and just what does your turning up mean?

As a child of God you have the Holy Spirit living within you and your very presence is good news to those who suffer. In 2 Corinthians Paul describes those of us who are Christians as 'a letter of Christ, cared for by us [Paul and Timothy], written not with ink but with the Spirit of the living God, not on tablets of stone but on tablets of human hearts' (3:3 NASB). These living letters can be 'known and read by all men' (3:2, NASB) and so it is impossible for us to hide and conceal the good news that lives within us. In Romans we read that the very feet of those who bring good news are beautiful (10:15), which is itself a quote from Isaiah where that idea is expounded: 'How lovely on the mountains Are the feet of him who brings good news, Who announces peace and brings good news of happiness, Who announces salvation, And says to Zion, "Your God reigns!"' (Isaiah 52:7, NASB). Your desire will be to embody the gospel wherever you go and particularly to present it in a deep and meaningful way to those whom you are called to transform.

Can you think back to the best letter (or email) that you have ever received? What did it contain? Did it come from someone who knew you well? Imagine that you are a letter written to those who are suffering and whom you are called to reach. What good news do they need to hear? What is the Holy Spirit telling you they need to know? Of course primarily they need to hear the gospel, the very word means good news that Christ died to save them, but what else? If you can break down the message to them into more detail, what would it say specifically to them? Most probably it would contain words to tell them that they are loved, that someone cares for them and that you notice and see them. Simply being noticed is joyous to those who believe they are unseen. It would most likely go onto tell them that there is hope and they can be restored. The Holy Spirit is the author of the letter written on your heart. As you crystallise the message, keep on inviting and allowing Him to write it with you.

Dear Fellow Traveller,

In the work of Women Without Roofs we have sought to bring a message to the women in our care that not just tells them they can be lifted out of poverty, as any secular charity may do, but that we desire to see them fully restored. We have come to understand that their poverty is far deeper than a lack of material possessions, but rather is a lack of experiencing the fruit of the Spirit shown towards them. For instance, many of them have been abused and raped rather than shown love, joy and self-control by the men around them. Of course we desire to see the fruit of the Spirit grow within them through the Holy Spirit, but first they need to receive them from others. Many of them don't even know what it is like to be shown goodness. We see this as the role of Women Without Roofs, and our message to them is that they are worthy of receiving those good fruits from those around them.

Hooray for Jesus!

Anna

Not all messages that we are called to deliver on God's behalf are so warm and comforting, as the writer of Hebrews tells us 'For the word of God is living and active and sharper than any two-edged sword, and piercing as far as the division of soul and spirit, of both joints and marrow, and able to judge the thoughts and intentions of the heart' (4:12, NASB). The message may also not be as obvious as we expect. Take human trafficking in India. On first consideration we could well assume that our message will be to the women in the brothels, telling them how much they are loved and that God cares for them and longs to see them free.

The root cause of human trafficking in India runs much deeper, though, and is due to the cultural corruption of marriage. As Christians we know that God designed marriage as a union of two people that is not only an economic and familial arrangement but where sexual intimacy is enjoyed too. In many parts of India this concept has broken apart and marriage is often arranged for purely economic and domestic reasons only. Once the marriage has been consummated and children have been produced, wives will encourage their husbands to leave them alone and purchase sex outside the marriage. Hence the huge brothels in India and the demand for trafficked girls. If you want to address trafficking in India then, your message may not only be to the victims, but may also be a message for the whole of society that restores the marriage ideal in society. How do you know which message to deliver? By keeping in tune with the Spirit, who writes on our hearts.

In 1 Corinthians, Paul reveals that he cannot help but preach the gospel he has been entrusted with (9:16). He is simply compelled to share it and does not want to stop anyway! This will become our desire too, to keep on passing on the message to others and never to stop.

Ask yourself

Try writing down the message, as revealed so far to you by God, that you believe you should deliver to the people you care for.

Pray

Pray that you will be compelled to share the gospel and your particular message of good news.

INVOLVING OTHERS

Transforming the world on your own is not nearly as much fun as changing it with a team of friends. This section explores how to engage others and how to avoid some pitfalls that you may encounter when working with different people. There are so many dark places in the world and not one of us can change everything, so getting more people involved in transforming the world is vital and necessary to see God's Kingdom expand and transformation come about.

Day 33: Journeying with your friends

As I sat down to begin researching and writing this section, a good friend sent me a lovely message reminding me that friendship is a gift from God. It is so true – our friends are precious, and clearly because they are close to us, very often we want to share our new passion to change the world with them. Being part of a close team of friends, transforming the world together, is an amazing experience. But not everyone is called to the same ministry, and it is very easy to become hurt if your close friend does not share your specific calling and enthusiasm for transforming the world.

Friends come with all sorts of inclinations and preferences and thank goodness they do, as without them my life would be so much duller. In my experience I find it impossible to predict which of my friends will get enthused about my work in Nepal and which won't. My situation is a little different to most people's because I have to keep making new friends: as an Army wife we move house every two years (of course I keep in touch with old friends too!) but on meeting someone who may be very warm and gracious it seems impossible to tell if they will want to join me in transforming the world. The timeframe also varies hugely. Some of my friends have jumped on board with supporting Women Without Roofs almost immediately, some have taken years, and some have never made a donation or asked me to tell them about what is happening in Nepal.

I am sure your experiences with your friends will be similar, and I urge you to cherish your friends and enjoy the different perspectives they bring. If you become very caught up with your calling and passion to change the world then you'll need some companions to support you and some others to talk to about different things and change the subject every once in a while.

Dear Fellow Traveller,

A wonderful friend of mine once gently complained that she did not feel that anyone else in our church cared about the particular problem that she was called to support people going through. It was an issue that had affected her own family when her first child was born. In one sense I think she was right, others in the church did not care about it as much as she did, but that did not mean they were not compassionate. The opposite was the case and almost everyone in the church was serving and ministering to other groups of people with different problems. There are so many problems in the world that we can't all tackle the same ones, we need to accept that our friends and our church will have different passions, priorities and callings upon them.

Compassionately,

Anna

There is great enjoyment when a team of friends comes together to transform the world so absolutely make sure you invite them to join you. You don't need to go on at them, but equally don't assume they won't be interested either and that your social life needs to be kept entirely separate from your calling. Solomon tells us in Proverbs that 'Iron sharpens iron, So one man sharpens another' (27:17, NASB), and who better than our friends to challenge us and bring out the best in us. Friends get to see us in every realm of our lives and we should strive to live with integrity before them. As mentioned on day 28, what we buy speaks about our integrity and priorities. If, for example, your friends see you buying and wearing cheap fashion from Primark or Walmart, yet hear you telling everyone you care about stopping child labour, they will be the first to challenge you on your commitment to the cause.

Above all, love and cherish those special friends that join you in your mission or whom you are able to join in with on their journey of transformation. Cheer each other on in your work just as John the Baptist was able to do for Jesus (John 3:29–30). Don't let your relationship become all about service, but ensure that you have some fun times too. There may be different seasons in your friendship but remember that 'A friend loves at all times' (Proverbs 17:17, NASB), and there is great delight to be had in spending time face to face with each other, even God chose to do that with Moses (Exodus 33:11). As the famous Margaret Mead quote reminds us 'Never doubt that a small group of thoughtful, committed citizens can change the world; indeed, it's the only thing that ever has', and if Jesus had a preference for a small group of twelve, who are we to disagree?

It is very likely that as you embark on your mission to change the world you will find new friends joining you. As a person with strong passions and who is devoted to a cause, you are extremely attractive to others so do not be surprised if new friends come to participate with you in the exciting work you are doing for God. Love and treasure each of them.

Ask yourself

Have you asked your friends to join you in changing the world? Who would you love to have alongside you? Make plans to tell them about what you are doing. Are you being appreciative enough of those friends that are already journeying with you?

Pray

Thank God for the gift of friendship and your friends. Ask Him to help you be a good friend who enables everyone around you to walk in all the good ways God has prepared for them.

Day 34: Your role in the church

_____

No church is perfect, yet Christ chose to die for it. That's how much He loves it and values it, in fact He does not even call the Church 'it' but refers to her as His bride (Ephesians 5:25, Revelation 22:17). When the Church operates as it should, it truly is beautiful, and even when there are flaws in a church, it is still possible to catch a glimpse of the stunning beauty that Christ died for.

Imagine the scene: your pastor calls you to the front one Sunday and tells everyone about the amazing work you are doing with an unseen people group that no one else seems to know about, let alone care for. He or she praises you for your saintliness and presents you with a large cheque to help you further your labour of love. Everyone listening wants to volunteer with you and for the next year or so you are inundated with offers of help. The applause for your efforts echoes around the building and you feel that you could carry on ministering forever.

Occasionally scenes like this do happen, but not all that often. Should we be taking credit for God's work anyway? So much of what Women Without Roofs has achieved is not down to me – God has ordered our every step – but the temptation to take the credit for Women Without Roofs can be overwhelming. It is likely that your church will take a while to recognise the calling on your life, and it can be right to do so: our works should be demonstrated by fruit and we ought to wait patiently for it to appear. Once it does, it's our job to give God all the glory for the transformation and growth that has occurred, and if you can do this without blowing your own trumpet it only adds to your saintliness, so don't worry about telling everyone what God has done! Simply make sure you keep on testifying to God's power to transform, your role is always to inspire the church to praise God and love Him more. In doing so it becomes more beautiful and its light shines brighter.

It is tough being a member of a church that is not yet involved in mercy and justice work and that may not give much priority to it. You will need to decide if your role is to bring that new focus to the church, so clearly biblically mandated in Isaiah 58, or if you need to find a different church to support you. No decision like this should be rushed into, the choice of which church body to be part of is critically important. However, if you choose to be the lone prophetic voice in your church community calling forth justice, that's not easy either, so think through your decision carefully.

Dear Fellow Traveller,

I am writing this just ten days after the huge earthquake in Nepal in 2015 and have so appreciated the global scale of God's Church, which has responded compassionately to desperate needs in Nepal. The local church you attend should also be able to connect you and ought to take every opportunity to be an active part of the global Church, which it is such a blessing to be joined with. Remember the Church exists for those outside of it to whom it calls 'come' (Revelation 22:17), and though it may feel like one, it is not a social club.

I was extremely saddened recently to hear a non-Christian friend recount a story of how a church our mutual Christian friend attends had behaved dreadfully and inappropriately. It was so distressing to hear a non-church goer attack the church for being awful, and this will probably colour her judgment of Christ and the church for many years. Our mutual friend should not have shared the information, galling though it was. Be careful how you talk about your church, we should honour it at every opportunity.

With love for the Church,

Anna

Your church is your home and can offer enormous support both practical and spiritual as you embark on transforming the world. Most denominations have policies that may be useful to you and from which you may be able to borrow wording, if appropriate, for your project (such as those concerning the protection of children and vulnerable adults). Most churches also offer training, and have access to conferences where you can learn from other people's achievements and mistakes. Tap into these as much as you can. I am often overwhelmed by all the areas in which the church is working and to which people have been called, these stories inspire me greatly. Beyond that, your church will be a source of volunteers who may be able to help you in your work. The leadership will hopefully offer to provide prayer cover and advice to you on your calling, and if completely stumped by a tricky situation you find yourself in, will just pray for you, and hopefully forego the advice!

Churches also offer varied opportunities to try out leadership in a safe, accountable environment. If you plan on starting something completely new with the people group you have in mind to transform, then do find out if there is a way you could initiate something within the confines of the church. This would allow you to practise the skills you will need later to strike out on your own with a less familiar crowd.

Your role is to keep the church informed about your passion to change the world and what you are doing to transform it. Above all, invite fellow church members to celebrate your successes with you, if people are flourishing and lives are being saved through God's grace, then let your church in on the party, it will encourage so many, and you will likely get the help you need as well.

Ask yourself

What opportunities does my church offer so that I can grow, learn and practise new skills? In what ways can I link with the global church? Am I keeping my church up-to-date with everything I am involved in? Are they able to pray for me in an informed manner and also celebrate with me?

Pray

Thank Jesus for His beautiful bride, the Church: reflect on everything you love about it. Confess any times you have not spoken well of it, or have treated your membership of it lightly. Pray for God to bless your church and to use you as a blessing in it and through it.

Day 35: Facing criticism

Making the world a better place is messy business, the problems themselves are involved and hard to define, and the solutions may appear obtuse and overwhelmingly difficult to implement. Often it is a case of two steps forward and many more back. All this can feel tough, so you may invite others to come and join you in your work to ease your load, but then they may criticise you for what you are doing and problems just get worse.

Criticism, to a certain extent, should be expected. As we considered on day 7, the very essence of our love for others is disquieting to some and challenges their own actions and priorities. They may unfairly turn their unease with what you are doing into criticism against you. It takes strength and discernment to see this form of criticism for what it truly is.

On the other hand, on day 11 we discussed how there are many different views on how best to help people, and it seems to me there is no single solution to the world's problems that fits all people everywhere. Criticism in these circumstances may therefore be warranted – it might be that the way in which you want to transform the world has some unanticipated negative consequences. In these instances the best response is to pray for grace to accept the criticism and also to pray that the person delivering the critique would do so out of love and in order to be constructive, rather than tear down what you have done. You have every right to ignore some people's criticisms if they are not constructive, and always seek a third opinion, from someone you both esteem, if there seems no way to resolve their argument with yours.

Even the greatest heroes of justice and mercy have met with criticism, including Jesus who was accused of being a glutton and fraternising with sinners (Matthew 11:19). Take Mother Teresa, for example. She was utterly devoted to caring for Kolkata's destitute in the final days of their lives. She was so committed to this cause that she turned down donations of medical equipment that might have extended the lives of her patients. The most famous instance occurred when she would not accept a kidney dialysis machine that had been contributed freely. She knew that one machine would not be enough; how would she and her nuns decide which of their patients to treat with it and which not to? She also knew that she was not qualified to run a hospital; her role was simply to love and care for the dying. In a broader sense Mother Teresa was also criticised for not addressing the systemic causes of poverty in India that led to the destitute dying on the streets. Some felt that her work, noble though it was, did not get to the nub of the issue. Against these critiques Mother Teresa did not waver from loving and caring for the dying, and though criticised for not 'expanding' her work, she showed incredible commitment to the vocation God had called her to.

We may not have such a clear vision from God about what we should we doing, yet we can take encouragement from Mother Teresa's story. If even she was criticised, we should also expect to face some negative responses to our work. Following Mother Teresa's example, we need to keep on pressing into God, by spending disciplined time with Him, so that our vision and calling becomes clearer and we can weigh up the criticism we receive with God-enabled discernment. Mother Teresa spent lengthy fixed periods in prayer and regularly fasted; she was extremely committed to her calling as a nun and was not a secular health visitor. We need also to recognise the limitations of our influence when we meet with disapproval: we do not control all, nor can we alter everything. It is also helpful to remember that we are most likely to have been called to do what we are good at and enjoy, so if we receive criticism for doing a bad job at something we hate, we need to take that back to God and check that is what He wants us doing.

Dear Fellow Traveller,

Women Without Roofs has rarely faced criticism, but we have had to endure some. Several years ago there was a Channel 4 programme about the plight of young widows in Nepal. We posted some of the stories of our women on the programme's website and were then contacted by another viewer who showed a desire in supporting us. We were excited at the time because we were at the early stages of planning to open a women's home (now Grace Women's Home) and this woman implied that she would donate a large amount to help us achieve this dream. No money ever came from her, but she continued to ask lots of questions and we thought she was extremely interested in Women Without Roofs. In time she agreed to sponsor a woman and wanted to send a parcel to this woman with gifts of clothing. Usually we wouldn't allow this, as we believe firmly in giving money to Nepal and spending it there so that the country's economy can be strengthened, and also because so many parcels go missing on their way to Nepal. Regrettably, I agreed to send the parcel for this woman and of course it went missing, I should have known better than to send it. The woman was furious with us, she couldn't understand that sending parcels to Nepal was a not a guaranteed process and accused us of stealing the parcel's contents ourselves. She intended to write to the Charity Commission, our governing body, immediately to complain about our conduct and report our supposed lies. It was a horrid time, and while it may seem a small incident, she was so vitriolic toward us it made us question everything we were doing.

Thankfully she never made the complaint to the Charity Commission and Women Without Roofs was advised to write to the Charity Commission immediately to let them know what had happened and explain our side of the story first. Though we had not stolen the goods in the parcel, we had acted wrongly by allowing this woman to dictate our actions in the hope of securing a large donation from her, and had not stuck to our own policies and protocol. The experience allowed us to clarify what we would and wouldn't do for our supporters and in the end I believe it was a positive experience for Women Without Roofs, though it certainly didn't feel like it at the time.

Learning,

Anna

Perhaps the greatest form of criticism we can face in trying to change the world is apathy, from those we are trying to change, or from our friends and family. In the cases mentioned above both Mother Teresa and we at Women Without Roofs were also being praised for our work by other people during the times we were criticised. Apathy, however, is completely draining and seems to suck away all love we have for others. It is very hard to love someone when we receive no love or even emotion back from them. Whilst our motivation in helping others shouldn't be for praise, it is hard if all our efforts go unnoticed and unappreciated. In these times we need to draw ever closer to God and seek Him for our sustenance and encouragement. He promises that the reward for our good works will be in heaven. Despite it being hard to keep our faith in His promises when we face criticism, we can be certain that He has sent His Holy Spirit to minister to and encourage us at every possible opportunity.

Ask yourself

Are you ready to be criticised? Do you have a firm vision of what God has asked you to do so that you can hold on to it through all the storms that may come?

Pray

Thank God for the vision and the calling He has granted you already. Pray that it may become deeper and richer. Ask Him to send the Holy Sprit and to provide people who can encourage and advise you when criticism comes.

Day 36: Keeping secrets

Though this section of the book is called 'Involving others', it may not actually be the right time for you to involve others just yet. Some plans are too wonderful to be shared immediately and need time to ferment and for your dreams to grow. Just like the first few special weeks of pregnancy, when often only the new mother and father know a baby is on the way, it is a special time for hope to build and the secret to be treasured. Similarly, a seed is covered in soil and the first stages of any plant's growth occur in the dark, where no one can see. When there is new life in the natural world, the first stages often occur in secret.

For those of you who are introverts and feel it strange to share everything that is on your hearts with others, keeping secrets may come naturally to you. If you are an extrovert, though, maybe you need to learn how to treasure and mull over what God has revealed to you before sharing it with the world. It is good to do this because some things are best done in secret and it blesses us to prize our calling and passions in our hearts before God asks us to bring them into reality. You don't have to tell everyone what you are up to, not just yet anyway, and He invites us to dream with Him for a little while. Imagine the excitement that goes into planning a surprise birthday party. God delights in our excitement as we plan with Him too.

We know that 'The secret things belong to the LORD our God' (Deuteronomy 29:29, NASB) and we also know from experience that only He knows how to create a baby in a womb and cause the smallest seed to germinate and grow into a tree. All these processes can not be mimicked by humans and are overseen exclusively by Him. Likewise He is the one who gives us our calling and passions, and plants the desire to change the world in us. He will nurture those longings, and it is my belief that if He has given you a desire to transform the world, He will not let that wanting go unsatisfied.

Dear Fellow Traveller,

Joseph of Arimathea was a secret believer in Jesus Christ as the promised Messiah, yet he was used in the biggest story of all time. God didn't demand that he broadcast what he believed to everyone he knew, but God trusted him to be involved and that when the time came he would act. Joseph of Arimathea collected Jesus' body after He had died and placed it in his own family grave. It was a dangerous move and one that would have bought Joseph and his family unwelcome attention from the authorities that had just crucified Jesus, secrecy was required.

Shh....

Anna

We too do not need to be loud about our commitment and intentions; we just need to act, with subtlety if necessary, when the command comes. Sometimes silence is necessary to protect those we wish to help, such as asylum-seekers or persecuted Christians, who need to be loved with discretion.

Despite the examples given above, it is possible to keep unhealthy secrets and to allow our dreams for the future to become self-centred fantasies. As Psalm 139:23–24 instructs, we should ask God to reveal to us the secrets of our own hearts 'Search me, O God, and know my heart; Try me and know my anxious thoughts; And see if there be any hurtful way in me, And lead me in the everlasting way' (NASB). Sometimes our dreams of helping the hurting become all about our own status and superhero qualities – we fantasise about how we will benefit and appear to others when we start making a difference.

If you find yourself in that place of fantasising about making a difference rather than actually doing so, or of doing it all for your own self promotion, then Paul's second letter to Corinthians contains advice for you. We are to surrender what is hidden in the same way that Paul says he had to: 'we have renounced the things hidden because of shame, not walking in craftiness or adulterating the word of God, but by the manifestation of truth commending ourselves to every man's conscience in the sight of God' (2 Corinthians 4:2, NASB). He explains that by sticking firmly to the truth we will be commended to men so there is no need to dream of and long for self-publicity. We are also warned that 'God will judge the secrets of men through Christ Jesus' (Romans 2:16, NASB). All this means that to beat our tendency to fantasise about changing the world alone, we need to search out truth and stick to it. Knowing the truth is likely to cause us to want to take action and whether we do so loudly and publicly, with the aim of drawing others into our mission, or quietly and in secret to protect those we are helping, will be revealed by Jesus Christ, the Truth.

This may sound rather mysterious, and perhaps it should be. Jesus himself spoke in parables and counselled His disciples that only those to whom God wanted to reveal the Kingdom of Heaven would understand and take hold of the truth in His parables. To others it would seem like downright foolishness. His parables have a logic all of their own and we learn the most when we remember that we are simply students of God's truth and have much to discover and be taught. He will choose how and when we are ready for His revelations; it is a privilege to understand the mind of God.

Ask yourself

Does God want you to keep your calling a secret for a little while so you can dream with Him and nurture your plans? Or, is it time to reveal your calling to others and invite them to join you?

Pray

Thank God for the dreams to transform the world that He has already placed in you. Pray that they would grow in a healthy way and that God's truth would nourish and sustain them. Pray for wisdom about when and how to reveal your calling – which up until now may have been a secret – to your friends and family.

Day 37: Encourage, encourage, encourage

Just as the famous mantra tells us 'location, location, location' is what's really important about buying a house, the key to keeping going with transforming the world is 'encourage, encourage, encourage'. Our work will flourish when we create an encouraging atmosphere around us. We will find it easy to encourage those we are blessing, those we are working with and hopefully, if the environment really is positive, some of that encouragement will come our way too. Churches should be centres of excellence for encouragement and so should our small groups. All of this encouragement is a blessing to God as well. Though He does not need it, He is still able to enjoy seeing us encouraged, and He sends His Spirit to help us minister encouragement to one another.

In the New International Version of the Bible the word 'encourage' does not appear until Acts. This is possibly a translation phenomenon, but from Acts onwards 'encourage' becomes a buzzword. Encourage is translated from the Greek word 'parakaleo' and is therefore only found in parts of the Bible that were translated from Greek, which is most of the New Testament. There may, however, be another reason: the Holy Spirit was sent to be an encourager and to give us the gift of encouragement (Romans 12:6–8). It was only after Jesus ascended to heaven, and we were left on our own in the world with the Holy Spirit, that encouragement has been so necessary to keep us going. Changing the world is not easy and we often need encouragement to even hold on to our faith in turbulent times.

The Old Testament, on the other hand, gives us some examples of poor encouragement. Job's friends only add to his despondency when they rally to him after he has lost family and fortune, and Proverbs warns us with salient metaphors that we need to be sensitive to others: 'Like one who takes away a garment on a cold day, or like vinegar poured on a wound, is one who sings songs to a heavy heart' (Proverbs 25:20, NIV).

Well-chosen words, whether written or spoken, can lift us up when we feel low. One of the trustees of Women Without Roofs often finishes her emails and telephone conversations with 'thanks for all you do'. She says it sincerely and it is lovely to be remembered and thanked each time I interact with her. Her little catchphrase never becomes tired, and though I have also seen it written in emails to others, it still takes an effort for her to write it each time and I know it is heartfelt. The biblical Barnabas also had a catchphrase: he repeatedly urges believers 'to be true'. Is there a phrase you could start using to regularly bolster others? We should feel under no pressure to be original when we encourage others: if we have to keep repeating the same message, maybe it's because our friends, co-workers and beneficiaries need to keep hearing it. The scriptures themselves are a great source of encouraging lines and verses and we are instructed to use them to bring about hope (Romans 15:4) – maybe you could borrow one to become your catchphrase.

Who is the most encouraging person you know? In the Bible, Paul is the master of encouragement and manages to encourage no matter what situation he finds himself in, even in prison he is there jollying everyone along. Whilst writing letters of admonishment he is still able to slip in some words to cheer on his readers, and the writer of Hebrews also draws a connection between discipline and encouragement in much the same way parents discipline their children (Hebrews 12:5). Paul recognises that all of us, at one time or another, need our faith encouraged: 'you and I may be mutually encouraged by each other's faith' (Romans 1:12, NIV) and repeatedly exhorts his readers to encourage one another (1 Thessalonians 4:18, Philippians 2:1) with specific words.

Dear Fellow Traveller,

I find this true in my own life, if I receive encouragement from someone who really knows me and understands what I am facing in detail, then the words they speak to me have much more effect than a glib sentiment. So also we should try to be specific when we give encouragement and make the effort to discern what it is the recipient needs to hear to overcome. Using an encouraging catch-phrase is the baseline for encouragement that we can build on with more specific words. Paul even wants Timothy to get in on the encouragement act and be like him, he encourages him to be an encourager, and so it becomes the gift that keeps on giving (2 Timothy 4:2).

Living in America as I write this is great, being honest, the people here say far more encouraging things than we Brits do. What I've realised though is that encouragement is not just about saying the right things, it's about our actions too and, as it goes, I think the British are actually pretty good at creating encouraging environments. It's no good giving someone some uplifting words if your actions go on to make them think you don't trust them (before I get into trouble, I'm not saying Americans are guilty of this). I know I undermine the encouragement that I give my children, I may tell them they'll be great at something and then proceed to ask them a hundred questions about whether they've remembered everything they need. Either I believe they can do whatever it is they are up to or I don't, and if I am going to encourage them I need to make sure all my actions back up that message.

You can be an encourager too,

Anna

Hebrews offers some hints about creating an affirmative environment. Firstly it says 'encourage one another daily' (Hebrews 3:13, NASB), encouragement therefore does not need to be spontaneously given; we can plan to say or do something encouraging each day and make it a discipline or rhythm of our life. Secondly, Hebrews invites us to 'consider how we may spur one another on toward love and good deeds, not giving up meeting together, as some are in the habit of doing, but encouraging one another' (Hebrews 10:25, NASB). Clearly, we need to be around each other if we are going to encourage one another. Paul gives some further advice to pay special attention to particular groups 'encourage the disheartened, help the weak, be patient with everyone' and tells Timothy to give careful instruction when encouraging (2 Tim 4:2). It will do us no harm to learn from these masters of encouragement.

Ask yourself

Whom could you call, email or text right now to offer some encouragement? What rhythms of encouragement could you introduce into your schedule to make encouraging others easier? Is there a catch phrase you could adopt?

Pray

Thank God for all those people in your life that encourage you. Ask Him to help you be more encouraging to others and to create a more affirmative environment when you are working to change the world.

Day 38: Tell your story, the next generation

Just as our world is so vast and its people so varied, so too time is long and the future needs to be changed as much as today does. There will be new challenges, of course, and some sins of oppression so prevalent today in society will be conquered. God is active in all of it: He is the Creator of history and His love for humankind never changes. Thinking about the long term, both forwards and backwards, is not always easy for us, but as long as we realise that God sees the larger picture and invite Him to guide us with the long term in mind, we will be on course with Him to transform the world and change history.

Mary, mother of Christ, caught a sense of this. In Luke 1 her astounding song of praise, the Magnificat, thanks God for choosing her to be Jesus' mother. Can you imagine Luke possibly sitting down with her and recording it many years later? What a conversation it could have been as they recalled memories of her pregnancy and Jesus as a baby in her old age. Maybe they never met, but possibly they did. In verse 48 we read 'From now on all generations will call me blessed' (NASB), and to me it seems that Mary understood and knew that the world had changed with Jesus' coming and that His arrival would never be forgotten; history and the future of humankind would be different forever. With humility, that should also be our aim as we set about trying to change the world. Hopefully our impact will be lasting, and that means inviting the next generation to become involved with us, otherwise our efforts will peter out.

Who are these other generations we should be speaking to? Our culture has developed a plethora of names for them, such as 'the baby boomers', 'Generation X', 'Generation Y', and 'millennials', and subscribes common characteristics to them. Are these supposed characteristics any more accurate than star signs or Chinese birth year attributes? Certainly technology plays a part in how different generations communicate, and our social history has a huge impact. The peace, love and sexual revolution of the 60s can be traced back to the end of the Second World War. The baby boomer generation, those born immediately after the second world war, were tired of hearing the war stories of their parents and craved an alternative life to that of their families which had been so dominated by war and sacrifice. They threw off social constraints and called for peace and love instead.

We should be cautious about giving too much weight to these generational stereotypes though. God remains the same throughout history, so does His love, and the human desire to be loved, valued and find meaning is likewise constant. Do not feel that your message and story needs to be altered or changed depending on your audience – everybody loves to hear someone who is authentic and who speaks truth, and who does not gloss over the bad and difficult parts.

Telling the next generation may not only mean telling those younger than you. As much as our individualistic natures may hate it, God perceives us in groups and often deals with us that way. There are countless examples throughout the Bible of God calling to and speaking to entire groups of people, whether they be defined by age, era, sin, race or ethnicity. Telling the next generation may mean that you tell someone who is different from you about what God is doing in your life and calling you to. Perhaps they will even be older than you. Make an effort therefore to ensure your home groups are made up of people from various backgrounds and that you at least occasionally help out with children's groups, the youth group, the older persons group and whichever other groups there are in your church. Tell some non-Christians too and make use of social media to get your story out.

Psalm 145 is the blueprint for how to tell the next generation. Verses 3 to 7 issue a calling to tell of God's work to future peoples: 'Great is the LORD and most worthy of praise; his greatness no one can fathom. One generation commends your works to another; they tell of your mighty acts. They speak of the glorious splendour of your majesty – and I will meditate on your wonderful works. They tell of the power of your awesome works – and I will proclaim your great deeds. They celebrate your abundant goodness and joyfully sing of your righteousness' (NIV). Looking at the verbs from this passage we should be praising, commending, telling, speaking, meditating, proclaiming, celebrating and singing about God so that the next generation knows how good He has been to us and what He has done in our lives and in the lives of others.

At church and at home groups I love to hear personal stories of how God is working in people's lives. If I am honest I much prefer these to hearing someone preach. Hearing a humble testimony from someone I know makes following Jesus so much more practical, yet also inspiring, and it is good to know other people have similar challenges and trials to me.

Dear Fellow Traveller,

When I was a child, at each Christmas morning church service we would telephone my pastor's twin brother in Nepal. (This was before the internet and Skype, so a lot of set up was required.) My pastor's name was Iain and his brother was Peter. Every Christmas morning we would hear stories of what it was like to celebrate Christmas in secret in Nepal, hear how they ate rice instead of turkey, and discover if they were able to meet together that year. These stories fascinated me, and years later it was Peter who introduced me to Eileen which led to the start up of Women Without Roofs. I am so thankful to Iain and Peter (and the people who set up the telephone and microphone on Christmas Day!) who took the time to share with me, and the congregation as a whole, how it felt to be spreading God's word in other countries. Peter never made it sound easy, or even all that exciting, he didn't get many presents or eat Christmas cake, but it was authentic and honest and his stories intrigued me. Know that it will bless others when they hear your stories of changing the world.

Faithfully,

Anna

Ask yourself

What is the story of your calling and passion to change the world? Where did it come from and how is God working in your life? What have you learnt so far? Who would benefit and be encouraged by hearing your story? Can you arrange to tell them?

Pray

Praise God for the work He is doing in your life and how He is using you. Pray that He would help you to remember all the small and big ways He is working with you. Ask Him to work with you to tell your story to the next generation.

Day 39: Holy rest!

Wait a minute; does the title for today mean we get to take a break from transforming the world? Yes, and no. God's calling on your life is ever constant and God may speak to you at any moment about it, even in dreams and visions whilst you are asleep. Yet in executing your calling and working to transform the world you need to adhere to God's own example when He created the world, and find time for rest. It is in periods of rest that our hurts heal too, just as a bridge is repaired at night when there is little traffic, so too our souls find healing when we commit to rest.

God commands us to keep the Sabbath in the Ten Commandments, so it seems that He takes our rest pretty seriously. It should be a pleasant command to keep, yet somehow it seems to be countercultural and we experience guilt when we take time out. Even telling other people that we are having time alone or admitting we are not busy for a few hours goes against the grain of our society. Consider these words written by Anne Morrow Lindbergh[39]: 'If one sets aside time for a business appointment, a trip to the hairdressers, a social engagement, or a shopping expedition, that time is accepted as inviolable. But if one says: I cannot come because that is my hour to be alone, one is considered rude, egotistical or strange. What a commentary on our civilisation, when being alone is considered suspect; when one has to apologise for it, make excuses, hide the fact that one practices it – like a secret vice!' Our society idolises busyness, we see confirmation of that in all those Facebook updates.

What does keeping the Sabbath mean then? And how do we do it? It is certainly not about being lazy; there are plenty of warnings in the Bible about the perils of being lazy or idle. Sabbath is a far richer experience and contains many depths. It is a serious business (or busyness) and requires discipline on our part to mark it and tear ourselves away from everything that seeks to distract us from God. We are not to simply empty our minds and clear our diary for a few hours, but to actively turn towards God and delight in Him. We may spend our Sabbath at church where we corporately delight in God and celebrate what He has done (see day 34) or we may practise Sabbath during the week when we find pleasure in Him, either alone or in a small group. Expressing our appreciation for God will involve prayer and worship, and at its most pleasurable can be described as playing with God. Just as a child and adult play together, we can have that same relationship with God our Father who longs for us to simply enjoy each other's company.[40]

Keeping Sabbath allows us to take a step back from the culture in which we spend most of our time, and look instead at God, the source of everything we need. Being in an unfamiliar environment is exhausting and we should not be surprised if as Christians we become fatigued from living in a world that does not hold Christian truths dear. Romans 8 describes the physical, mental, spiritual and emotional pain that we experience living in a world that is not yet fully redeemed; it is no wonder that we need a break from time to time. Our time with God will leave us renewed and strengthened, ready to take on the next challenge with Him. We will achieve far more like this than if we never turn towards Him.

In our mission to change the world, observing the Sabbath means also taking a pause in our work for God. It is about leaving the changes we desire to see for God to achieve in His own time, firmly believing that all things are in His hands and not up to us alone. This is a theological statement of trust and obedience that admits God loves and longs to see change in people's lives even more than we do. If we never take a break from changing the world we may fall into the trap of believing all the changes we see are solely down to us.

Paradoxically, we have to work at keeping the Sabbath, but the rewards are huge both for us and those we are hoping to help. In order to rest successfully we may need to make some rules. Within *Work, Play, Love* by Mark Shaw[41] there are some great game strategies for helping us to enjoy life more. They are well worth attempting, though you will need an egg timer! Our Sabbath rules may be simpler than the game and its rules described in the book. We need to set time aside for God so that we can hear from Him, devote ourselves again to Him and spend time getting to know Him better. All of this is done so that we can carry out His mission on earth with more clarity, purpose and energy, having rested.

Dear Fellow Traveller,

International Justice Mission staff tell how they are required to pray at their desks for half an hour at the start of each day. The result has been a huge expansion in their influence and the number of rescues. IJM employs highly driven staff who passionately desire the end of human trafficking. Their caseloads can be overwhelming so it might seem counterproductive to stop and pray, yet their work has flourished.

Pausing,

Anna

We may struggle with stepping away from our work because for many of us our identity is caught up with changing the world. We long to be known as the 'supersaint' who does great things for others, but in making time to play, pray and delight in God we leave behind our pride and enjoy being a child of

God again. Our identity in Christ is not defined by what we do for Him, but in what He has done for us on the cross, and practicing Sabbath is a declaration of this identity.

Ask yourself

Do I idolise busyness? Do I ever say I am busy when I am not, or overly emphasise my workload to others? What rules and principles could I introduce so that I observe the Sabbath and make time for God in my week? Is my identity bound up in what I do for God rather than what He has done for me?

Pray

Ask God to help you rebel against the idolisation of busyness in our society. Pray that you would be released from the guilt of not being busy every once in a while. Thank God that our identity is found in Him alone.

Day 40: Do not forget to love

This is the final day of our journey, but there is so much more ahead for you to delight in as you work with God to transform situations and the lives of the needy. It is as if you have reached the end of spring board, and now you dive in, or maybe it feels more as if you have climbed a mountain, the hang-glider is strapped to you and now it is time to launch yourself into the sky. The adventure has barely begun.

The starting point for this journey was an acknowledgement that so much is wrong with the world and that it is not as God intended it to be. These words sum up the position we found ourselves in:

'We pray to God because He has too much to answer for to be allowed simply to disappear, because we have to protest against Him as well as to Him, and because the only alternative is despair, or silence.'[42]

God answers our prayers by involving us in His plans to transform the world and promises that we will find rich rewards in doing so. No greater delight can be found than working alongside God in bringing about His eternal purposes. His assurances mean that no matter how messy our lives are and what baggage we bring with us, He can use us and heal us. His message is that 'in all things God works for the good of those who love him, who have been called according to his purpose' (Romans 8:28, NIV).

This calling and fulfilment is what the world yearns for, we see evidence of this in the high numbers of men and women who have travelled to Iraq and Syria to fight with Isis. Life in the West offers little significance and is full of meaningless frivolities; young people are rarely offered a cause to give their all to. Isis fills this void and it is now time the church gives a riposte; living for God and carrying out His purposes is exciting, fulfilling, has eternal impact and most of all our life can count if we give it to Him.[43]

Our passion to see the world changed is driven by love, and the key to continuing in the works and calling that this book has stirred in you is to keep asking for God to give you more love. As Corinthians 13 repeatedly warns us, if we carry out even the very best ideas by merely our own efforts, and do not have love, we are nothing more than clanging symbols (perhaps the analogy today would be white noise). Love is immensely powerful, it has the power to topple governments and restore the darkest hearts.

Trying to change the world on our own without God is like working in the dark. To our eyes the attempts look bright and meaningful, yet when God brings His glory to a situation it is like the dawn rising over a city. Imagine for a moment New York or London at dawn: both cities appear so vibrant during the darkness, but look somewhat grimy and ordinary when daybreak comes. Similarly, our efforts that look so brilliant in the night pale into insignificance against the bright sun that is God's love and power to bring transformation and healing. To work without God is to miss out on His dazzling goodness and love, both for us and those we are seeking to assist. When we position ourselves on the front lines of God's work in the world, and He shows up, we begin to see miracles happen.

Dear Fellow Traveller,

Though not guaranteed, my prayer for you, now that you are a world-changer, is that you see the fruit of your works. Just as Paul wrote to the Ephesians, I pray that in joining with God in His mission to transform the world you are able 'to grasp how wide and long and high and deep is the love of Christ' (Ephesians 3:18, NIV). May God overwhelm you with both grace to love others and a deep awareness of His goodness. When problems arise, I pray that you are able to recall that His love is unquenchable and irrepressible. As time progresses may He let His calling on your life become ever clearer.

With hope for a transformed world,

Anna

And finally, let us never forget that His love wins.

Pray

Pray for more love.

Acknowledgements

In my view, the most valuable aspect of this book is the listening exercise carried out in the first fortnight, yet I can not claim credit for it. Instead I am incredibly grateful to Amanda Rose who gently led me through the process and has allowed me to share it with you. She also encouraged me to write and to find my own mission in the world. These few words are not enough to acknowledge her generous input in my life, yet I hope they will suffice for now and that we can be 'on the same soil', whether in Jamaica, the UK, or elsewhere again soon.

My thanks goes to Eileen Lodge who invited me to be part of the story of godly transformation in Nepal. The trustees of Women Without Roofs are a wonderful and generous set of people, they have allowed me to follow my dreams and have put up with a few hare-brained ideas on the way, all whilst keeping within the rules of the Charity Commission and the IRS (which is a far more onerous beast). Much of the wisdom contained in this book is actually wisdom passed on from them.

No matter where we live in the world, our home church has always been Dayspring, a place where it is safe to think differently and try to find new paths to follow God. There are many people there who have stuck with us through near and far, good times and bad. Without their solid support and foundation, we would be lost and we always look forward to worshipping again with them and seeing where God is leading them.

In America I have been blessed to find a Christian editor living next door to me, this book has been immeasurably improved by Amanda Rooker's feedback and encouragement. God proved His phenomenal ability to connect people across time and continents again. The incredible Jess Reeve has done a fantastic job designing the book cover and I am grateful for her good advice.

I would like to acknowledge the loving environment that my family has provided: my grandparents Audrey and Maurice for loving each other faithfully for many years and my grandparents Jean and Ron for demonstrating commitment to causes over generations. My parents Marilyn and John authentically continue this path, and I admire my sister Katie for the amazing grace she applies in her life day after day. My son Zach inspires me to solve the problems of the world – I know he will go on to solve many himself – and my daughter Bethany is deeply compassionate, she already feels the pain of others and will go on to love and serve many. My husband Simon is my greatest supporter and I am truly thankful that he is my husband; his generosity in allowing me to try to transform the world is the best gift anyone on earth has ever given me.

Thank you for reading this book

If you would like to donate towards the work of Women Without Roofs in Nepal then please visit:

mydonate.bt.com/charities/womenwithoutroofs-nepal

Notes

[1] Anna Townsend is the founder and chair of trustees of Women Without Roofs – Nepal, a charity that supports women who face hardship in Nepal (www.wwr-nepal.org). It is registered in the UK with the Charity Commission under registration number 1132931 and in the USA with the IRS under EID 47-2053956.

[2] Celtic Daily Prayer (The Northumbria Community Trust (2000), *Celtic Daily Prayer*, London: HarperCollins) is a excellent resource and contains a two-year daily Bible-reading plan as well as a rich selection of prayers and readings.

[3]de Foucauld, Charles, (1930), 'Prayer of Abandonment', *Meditations Day 4*, Celtic Daily Prayer (The Northumbria Community Trust (2000), *Celtic Daily Prayer*, London: HarperCollins)

[4] A longer version of this story is available at http://onelifesofar.wordpress.com/about-us/annas-story/.

[5] Lourde (2013), 'Tennis Court' from *Pure Heroin* [CD] New Zealand: Universal

[6] In Ireland, the country with the highest childbirth safety record, only one woman in 47,600 will die in childbirth. Source: Kristoff, N and WuDunn, S (2009), *Half the Sky*, New York: Knopf.

[7] Stop The Traffick is running an excellent campaign to tackle the injustices of the Sumangali apprentice scheme in Tamil Nadu, India where 200,000 girls are trafficked in order to make clothes for high streets around the world.

[8] See Campolo, T and Darling, M (2007), *The God of Intimacy and Action*, San Francisco: Jossey-Bass.

[9] Foster, R (2008), *Celebration of Discipline: The Path to Spiritual Growth*, London: Hodder & Stoughton.

[10] BBC World News on BBC Four provides excellent coverage and analysis of worldwide problems.

[11] A full explanation of Lectio Divinia is contained in Campolo, T and Darling, M (2007), *The God of Intimacy and Action*, San Francisco: Jossey-Bass.

[12] There is much more about Poustinias in Doherty, C (1998), *Poustinia: Encountering God in Silence, Solitude and Prayer*, Canada: Madonna House.

[13] Ibid.

[14] See page 100 of Foster, R (2008), *Celebration of Discipline: The Path to Spiritual Growth*, London: Hodder & Stoughton.

[15] Bonar, H (1995), *Words to Winners of Souls*, Phillipsburg: P & R Publishing

[16] Keller, T (2010), *Generous Justice*, London: Hodder & Stoughton.

[17] Putnam, RD and Campbell, DE (2010) *American Grace: How Religion Divides and Unites Us*, New York: Simon & Schuster

[18] An excellent movement to inspire Christians to get involved in politics is being run by Christians in Politics. Various events have been organised and their message is contained in Flannagan, A (2015), *Those Who Show Up*, Edinburgh: Muddy Pearl

[19] Lewis, CS (1950), The Lion, the Witch and the Wardrobe, London: Geoffrey Bles.

[20] 'Prayer of Caedmon', Celtic Daily Prayer (The Northumbria Community Trust (2000), *Celtic Daily Prayer*, London: HarperCollins)

[21] List taken from Greer, P (2015), 'Stop helping us! Moving beyond charity to job creation'

Business as Mission: businessasmission.com/stop-helping-us.

[22] Trickle-down economics is a whole field of study.

[23] Why it is that microcredit, lauded for dramatic poverty reduction in the developing world, is not used in developed countries to relieve poverty? It would be fascinating to see the outcome of a community savings and loan group implemented for instance amongst young unemployed people in a deprived city within the UK. How about a television documentary about a microcredit group in the UK? I'm sure the results would be fascinating. David Lammy MP noted in a speech that entrepreneurial young people growing up in some inner cities turn to selling drugs because there is no small business start-up support or training.

[24] Take a look at www.mdrc.org for a good example of how research influences social solutions in the USA.

[25] See books by Jeffrey Sachs, Paul Collier, Laurence Smith, etc.

[26] Chimamanda Ngozi Adichie's well-researched novels are a great example of how stories can explain cultural history.

[27] More information on the Cinnamon Network and Matt Bird, the founder, is at cinnamonnetwork.co.uk.

[28] Koshish Nepal, run by Matrika Devkota, does phenomenal work on a shoestring. They have the only home for mentally ill women in Nepal, and Matrika's phone rings off the hook. They are in desperate need of funds, if you can donate please go to koshishnepal.org/pages/donate-support.

[29] fairtrade.org.uk

[30] Try ethicalsuperstore.com.

[31] If you care about the people who make your clothes then Labour Behind the Label, based in Bristol, produces some useful reports – see www.labourbehindthelabel.org. I particularly love People Tree's fair trade clothing range – see www.peopletree.co.uk.

[32] tjm.org.uk

[33] A good overview of trade between countries and how it could work to promote development can be found in Stiglitz, J and Charlton, A (2007) *Fair Trade For All* Oxford: Oxford University Press.

[34] Global Justice Now was formerly known as the World Development Movement

[35] Available from Sainsbury's and The Co-operative supermarkets.

[36] A discussion on Evangelical Americans' attitude to environmental issues can be viewed here: billmoyers.com/episode/climate-change-faith-and-fact.

[37] For example, the founders of EcoScraps and Republic Services are multi-millionaires.

[38] Eileen Lodge's story is contained within the INF book *Light Dawns In Nepal* available from the INF website: inf.org/news/inf-international/story-inf.

[39] Gift From The Sea, Anne Morrow Lindbergh, Pantheon, 1991

[40] For more on the idea of playing with God, see Shaw, MR (2014), *Work, Play, Love*, Nottingham: IVP

[41] As above.

[42] Celtic Daily Prayer, Aidan Readings, May 21 (The Northumbria Community Trust (2000), *Celtic Daily Prayer*, London: HarperCollins)

[43] See this video that offers brotherly love to Da'esh/Isis from The People of the Cross: youtu.be/uSv4vBcFyvo.

13957851R00088

Printed in Great Britain
by Amazon.co.uk, Ltd.,
Marston Gate.